sidebrow
01

Sidebrow 01
ISBN: 0-9814975-0-0
ISBN-13: 978-0-9814975-0-1
©2008 by Sidebrow

Cover art: "Meditation on a Brick Ship" by Andrew Schoultz
Cover & book design: Jason Snyder
Printing: McNaughton & Gunn

Sidebrow
912 Cole St., #162
San Francisco, CA 94117

sidebrow@sidebrow.net
www.sidebrow.net

A Member of

Inter section
incubator
Services for Artists
www.theintersection.org

Sidebrow is a member of the Intersection Incubator, a program of Intersection for the Arts (www.theintersection.org) providing fiscal sponsorship, networking, and consulting for artists. Intersection is San Francisco's oldest alternative arts space, presenting groundbreaking works in the literary, performing, visual, and interdisciplinary arts.

Contributions and gifts to Sidebrow are tax-deductible to the extent allowed by law.

sidebrow
01

SIDEBROW

San Francisco

2008

acknowledgments

Sidebrow would like to acknowledge the generous support of the following individuals for their founding donations:

Jeff & Laurie Kamerer

Matthew McGlincy

Celeste Schaefer Snyder

Dan & Linda Snyder

Sidebrow would also like to thank the following individuals for their generous support in bringing this anthology to press:

Oliver & Ruby Bettinger • Nicole Bratt • Justin Brown

Scott & Kerri Carlson • Dominic Cesario • Christopher & Evelyn Cleary

Dan Gellar & Dayna Goldfine • Shayne Haynes & Sara Tamarin Haynes

Geraldine Kim • Kimberly Leja • John & Marilyn Leja

Dennis & Rebecca Lyu • Michael Mackenzie • Chris McCaman

Donald Murawski & Steve Magnani • Judith Nihei • Michael Rolf

Seth Rosenthal & Maia Rosal • Kelleren Snyder

Dave & Sydney Szumski • Anonymous

sidebrow
01

Jenny Allan • A.K. Arkadin • Jeff Bacon • Andrea Baker

Julia Bloch • Lawrence Ytzhak Braithwaite • Nick Bredie • Amina Cain

Kate Hill Cantrill • Nona Caspers • Jimmy Chen • Kim Chinquee

John Cleary • Steve Dalachinsky • Catherine Daly • Brett Evans

Brian Evenson • Raymond Farr • Sandy Florian • Paul Gacioch

Anne Germanacos • Scott Glassman • Noah Eli Gordon • Paul Hardacre

HL Hazuka • Anne Heide • Malia Jackson • Carrie-Sinclair Katz

Susanna Kittredge • Richard Kostelanetz • Kristine Leja

Norman Lock • Doug MacPherson • Scott Malby • Bob Marcacci

Bill Marsh • rob mclennan • LJ Moore • Greg Mulcahy • Cathi Murphy

Eireene Nealand • Daniel Pendergrass • Kristin Prevallet

kathryn l. pringle • Stephen Ratcliffe • Francis Raven • AE Reiff

Daniel C. Remein • Elizabeth Robinson • Zach Savich • Len Shneyder

Nina Shope • Kyle Simonsen • Ed Skoog • Jason Snyder

Anna Joy Springer • Chris Stroffolino • Cole Swensen • Joanne Tracy

Chris Tysh • Nico Vassilakis • James Wagner • Derek White

Joshua Marie Wilkinson • Angela Woodward

MOTHER, I

PROJECT

Each Sidebrow piece is affiliated with a thematic project. For information about a particular project, turn to the appendix at the back of the book.

1

2: p154 • 3

3: p162 • 1

SIDENOTES

Sidenotes provide alternate paths through the text. In addition to encouraging diverse readings, sidenotes highlight connections for creative response. Alternate paths are represented in page notation: For example, sidenote 2, at left, offers an alternate thread beginning on page 154 at sidenote 3. Notes without page notations (e.g., 1 and 5, at left) are points of entry for alternate readings offered elsewhere in the book. In many instances, sidenotes relay to sidenotes that relay to other sidenotes, offering interconnections among multiple pieces throughout the book.

4: p98 • 6

5

6: p149 • 1

CONTRIBUTOR

An appendix at the back of the book contains a full list of each author's contributions. Biographical information can be found at www.sidebrow.net/2006/contributors.php.

CHRIS TYSH

preface

This inaugural Sidebrow anthology offers both a snapshot of an ongoing collaborative experiment and an invitation to participate in its evolution.

Launched on the Web in 2005, Sidebrow was established to explore collective resonances among innovative works of poetry and prose. We have used the Internet as a tool for opening up the publishing process, launching thematic projects and working to facilitate creative response to pieces curated on the Sidebrow Web site. Interconnections among diverse contributions—both intentional and incidental—have emerged over time to open myriad possibilities for the formation of multiple-author, cross-genre books.

This anthology is a first step toward that effort. It is one possible iteration of an endeavor that is continually evolving. The sequence of the pieces included in this book introduces one path for reading it. Ongoing Sidebrow projects, listed in the appendix at the back of the book, introduce others. Sidenotes in the margin (see explanation, opposite) unveil additional means for navigating the book. These avenues are not exhaustive. We welcome your insights and input into the evolution of this endeavor and invite you to extend, reimagine, and otherwise respond creatively to what you see developing.

For new posts, emerging projects, and information on submitting work to Sidebrow, visit www.sidebrow.net.

Jason Snyder

John Cleary

Kristine Leja

Sidebrow Editors

sidebrow
01

[2nd & Mission]

Chance encounters, she whispers.

They are standing together close enough for him to hear her whisper above the din of onlookers crowding the street, and though, among them, he feels the edge of his attention—the heads just out of focus craning to see past him to the body on the sidewalk beyond—luring him to look away from her mouth, something about the thin curve of her lips holds him there, suggests she does not care whether he believes she has said this for him. Her eyes are glazed. The threat they pose, he thinks, remains hidden, dormant within. You will, you will not let her in.

Behind him, the gurney is loaded. Beneath the cloak, the body is thin. It is not for her, she feels, this body, this aftermath, this fallen man. Her attention is set squarely on him. She feels his silence as an assurance. His expression has not changed, and yet the constancy, the steeled eyes, the staid brow, his tightly drawn lips, awakens within her the pleasurable desire to wait for a place inside him to open so she can seep in.   *1*

I won't sleep with you, she whispers, *if that's what you think this is.*   *2*

He likes the way her smile suggests she saves it for moments like this.

The sirens have quieted. Lights flash. Red flushes alternating on her face and his.

Sex and death, he says. *Sex and death.*

Heat rises in the stem of her throat when he repeats it.   *3: p39 • 4*

Have I forgotten to ask if we've met?   *4*

His smile is sheepish. It is enough for her to get past this.

She looks at the gurney to avoid what she feels of his eyes. The hosing of blood off the sidewalk. The sound it makes at the drain. To get away from yourself for a time.

That sure was a trip.

He likes the nonchalance of her tone, the fast times and flippancy beneath this.

A fall, really, he replies.

His straight face, enigmatic in a way she likes. The intimation of sociopathology beneath its surface, drawing her always, the live wire she feels running through that long line of men.   *5: p44 • 7*

Not so sure he was committed to dying, he says.   *6*

She gestures to the spray of the hose, feels herself letting go as she watches the blood in dilution stream over the curb's lip.

How can you fake a commitment like that?

He has not taken his eyes off her. Watch yourself, she thinks.

Commitment is for the trees and the earth, he says.

We are rootless, he says. *We have no means to commit.*

The flash of self-consciousness he feels at having so soon laid it on so thick.

For a time, they stand silently before one another, he and she, in the street, and then the halo of space that surrounds them is broken as together they press through the crowded scene. What they had been, set apart, is lost among the bodies of strangers straining to witness the gurney as it is taken in. The doors of the ambulance open. The cloak shivers on entry. What is beneath appears thin.

Halt,

Small bone in transit. Still your odds in an orderly pile, some view.   *1: p42 • 1*
One bead aids advance. I didn't ask for circulation. Continue on,
I measure no less, until all liquid loses shape. That shiner of a
reminiscence. Me, wounded, approaching at the next station.   *2: p62 • 1*

Curiousier

Scene 50. Int. Late morning. Hansi's apartment.

A pretty young maid ushers Pierre in:

MAID

Madame has asked me if you wouldn't mind waiting a bit...

Pierre sinks deeper into the dusty rose damask, his thoughts a wild tumult igniting his suspicions about Hansi. Is he really thinking she's for hire: those hasty appointments, the feeble excuses, that insolent laughter in the taxi? Could it be he's already itching to be black and blue, bruised to the core, bits of skin raised to meet the blood? But what has the camera tracked? A sweaty *jeune homme* in a salon waiting for his Galatea to come to life? The director's dilemma is to film the unfilmable;

1: p162 • 9

to imbue this seemingly anodyne narrateme—the lover waits—with a rip, which will skim the top and glide across all that barbarous privilege of the living. How s/he manages to project Pierre's private carousel, where one minute Hansi forms the very emblem of passion—the girl he falls in

2: p64 • 2

love with—the next, that little bitch according her whip, will tilt the scene and make deeper the hole one must climb out of.

3: p192 • 3

Possibly, a silent digital projection could run high above eye level as if a decorative band or architectural detail that Pierre is absent-mindedly watching while smoking. The actors' resemblance to Hansi and our hero should be somewhat suspicious.

4: p25 • 1

Music over the scene.

[W. 3rd & MacDougal]

as if he were playing the music   on his skin   *1: p26 • 3*

  hair tangled   wire

      case made   orange in black   orbit of choices

  sympathetic cord   red i   cu   lous in conjunction with dynamic

                                    snap the

way wrists refuse to bend

as if my ears were the changes   addressed

        don't make up what's right in front of you   hot   mustard

salad

BITTER chorus' soured candy broken

heart

not yet thru the sketches   & the scribe's already in my BLOOD

feet of buzzards waiting in head

pounding eyes

saying Come to Me   come TO mE   (wish i had

a camera

that could make people real)

tripping over organic step

having less choice than will/string allows   incarnate

rooted in bulb

1: p194 • 4   keep "I" out of

rational choices

because museums allow such a thing

as if played the mass

2: p213 • 1   your pockets full o' theories

the basic combination of movements

the eventual ride home

sealed walls   unhinged

if i never saw that face again

i would blessit take the juice away   (improvise within   *1: p132 • 1*

the vocabulary

& fleece the sadly rumor   of

the particular language

but the time for invention is never gone

 you are speaking)

& thrives it like an old tongue

thru an intricate series of bailed canals

        it's a basin in here   a self-created cistern of dark

was L i gh t   once

                a bowl of delectable condiments

        even now with temperaments awash & the whole meal sampled   *2: p198 • 5*

for FREE.

Curiousier,

1

2

Caught in the Gunnersbury train. Stack yourself against the window. Your voice rides the length of me. *Two eyes serve a movement.* Would empty veins for. Greyish bruise above the pisiform. It's not your memory, it's you. Bloody coming up.

3: p161 • 1

Halt

Dear T,

1

However it could have went in Paris, years ago, in the night, drunk, along streets with willing women, paying, and the three hoods in the offshoot of the alley, while I turned to look as I left.

2 : p27 • 2

Uncertainty in their eyes—they seemed to be dealing—but I turned my head and walked back out into the main street.

I remember a bar later on, and watching a British comedy on a television with two Asians drinking beside me. They laughed at all the wrong times, or so it seemed to me.

I woke up with blood on my pillow, and glass in my hand.

3: p92 • 2

[Waller & Downey]

What have you got yourself into, she says, low to herself, but he can tell by her tone she wants him to hear her speak to herself like this.

1   The crosstown away from the suicide. The side street. The latch of the gate. The porch of a house he has told her is his. And how without fear she had fallen asleep, passed out on the bus, an

2   afternoon of drinking, a morning of drinking, an all night from she didn't know when before she

3   had seen that man fall, had met him in the swim of the crowd, had left with him to take the bus, to be with him, to keep it going, her head on his shoulder as she rested in blackness, the slow burn of danger and excitation of losing herself and curling into his arm without even knowing him.

She is looking at the black plastic sheet covering the lone picture window from inside. Creases in the plastic, a black web of broken lines. The sun, behind them, setting. The black plastic flashing dark red. What she has seen today, what she is seeing now with him on a porch she has never been

4: p39 • 5   to sends a chill down through her she likes.

Inside, the house appears even smaller, even more claustrophobic than it had from outside. The living room adjacent to the foyer. The kitchenette; its short, dividing countertop. Black plastic duct-taped over every window. The dark mouth of the hallway to unknown rooms. The whole of

5: p164 • 2   it a sick sweetness and sweat, oozing glands, milk from a mother's breast skinning in the ladle of a metal spoon. Except for the loveseat, the film projector, the metal shelf of film canisters along the

6: p156 • 1   wall, there is little to suggest that living occurs in this room.

7: p195 • 10   She feels the skin kiss of her thighs beneath her skirt. Images of herself, any one of innumerable unknown men, the thrill of dissolving into the intimate suggestions of unfamiliar rooms. There is a sterility here that she likes. Dim light from the kitchenette. The film projector gleams like a knife.

Fucking creepy if you ask me, she says.

Her smile again. He could melt into it, lose himself in the dark slit she offers, the moistness of her lips in the light. He forgets the fear that has flashed hot along the curve of his skull at his having brought her here, of her seeing into him like this, knowing his life in the hints of this space as he watched her open the empty cabinets before finding the one beneath the sink where the vodka is.

Other people's home movies are a mirror, he hears himself say despite his earlier vow to keep

8: p192 • 3   himself from laying it on too thick. *It's a way to reflect your own life without really seeing into it.*

She takes him in, and it is as if she is suddenly waking from the blackness into something she will forever remember, such is the odd weight she feels of the bottle cradled in her arms.

He has a face, the gauntness of which seems eroded. She feels for him suddenly, tingles with a fear that has not taken hold of her for some time. The way he holds her so patiently in his eyes makes her long to feel herself whole deep within him, to turn him inside out, to rape the hard line he makes of his mouth with her tongue.

She unscrews the vodka and feels herself settling.

You're one sick puppy, she says, *peeping into other people's lives without anything of your own on the line.*

She is a nurturer, he thinks, reading beneath this line.

You'd be surprised at what you find.

They are standing in the kitchenette, she with the bottle of vodka in her hand, he with a film canister held against his chest with crossed arms. There is a feeling of domesticity to this. A hint of intimacy and comfort. A Bauhaus rendition of man and wife that he likes.

WIVING

1

I am a duet with you
and tripled with you.

A wife in the corner
and you in the corner

beginning.

...

What grabs me is her ankle
caught from under the bedsheet
in my grip.

She can suggest a movement but cannot make it,

I can hold this near
miss but she can bear it.

...

Walking into the bedroom,
"of course there is no chair in here
                 and where will I sleep"
and what will I build.

1: p103 • 3

…

He calls her with the same sound

as he calls into his sleep,

she cuts away his excess

sound at night.

…

He has made her children round
enough to seal them
in his house, they fit there
and she is in the garden.

1: p101 • 1

…

This shape is scarce
because it is hers.

2: p64 • 1

She is an updraft and caught.

…

She would heave under you
the same way with red hair
and blank fingers.

She would heave under you
and ask you to spell her
out of this.

…

I am waiting in the parlor for you
I am waiting to make you wife

…

If this is not her mark, where do her feet fall   1: p191 • 1
where will she sleep that can make a mark.

As my soaped hands would show you
I am ready to cut   2: p165 • 6

her image sleeps against every surface
she can press.   my   sleep.

I have mistaken you for foliage.   (again)

ORPHÉE

1   The underworld, a dark hallway littered with debris.

2   The bedroom, where they always return.

3: p198 • 7   Small window, quilted spread, long mirror.

      All spaces are enclosed.

4   Where a man and a woman come in and out, very quickly: a departure.

      Where a woman re-enters: a transitional space.

5: p151 • 2   A man creates a space, but refuses to live in it.

6: p37 • 1   A woman occupies the space, because she remembers inhabiting it as a child.

      If she had treated him differently, would she have noticed that he was not an angel?

      This was what existed: the robins on the edge of the pond.

      This was how it ended: the centipede caught in a rug.

      This is how it evolved: the faucet running down brick.

      Is it a question of what's dead?

7   The ecstasy of saints is the realization that they are water.

libido spectandi

the convulsionaries of saint medard appear before him, their bodies covered in wounds. their deacon dead. the men drag the body behind them on a funeral bier. the women gather at the grave site, clumps of hair clotted in their hands—patches torn out with the scalp attached. their cheeks riven with scratches, their breasts bruised. the women fling themselves to the ground, bodies prostrate before the grave, limbs flailing into seizure. as the men drag the deacon nearer, their heels hit the ground hard. the rhythm, a dirge driven into the dirt. the women succumb to ecstasies, eating the earth around the tomb, calling out for cures. they bark and mew, leap in the air, strike themselves with axes, spades, hammers, swords. showing one another how they do not bleed. the women twist their nipples with pliers, stick their breasts with pins, until they look like barbed and armored beasts. waiting for the men to trample them into earth.

1

2: p30 • 3

STUNG

His stepfather's body was genuflected as if disposed at prayer, a bee wriggling on it, its stinger inserted into the naked back. The boy took a pillow from the bed, slid his hands inside the pillowcase, used the pillow to push the body over. His stepfather teetered and fell, crushing the bee beneath him. The mouth of the fellow had been sewn shut with carpet thread, which had begun to tear out through the lips. The hands and feet were swollen, and the face was so puffy that the cheeks overwhelmed the eyes—two squinting slits sunk deep into flesh.

The boy used the pillow to move the arms around a little. He took his hands out of the pillow and put it on the knees and sat, hearing the knees crack when they slowly straightened beneath his weight. He sat there staring down at the body. The carpet thread had been sewn in blood-tipped cross-stitch all the way along the lips, nine stitches in all, the outer two torn all the way through so that there was an exit through which a bee, its wings plastered back against its abdomen, could, and did, squirm.

Through the glass doors he saw his mother lying on her towel, her bare back up, her head hidden beneath a bleached, floppy straw hat. He hesitated, until he saw her move.

He slid the door open.

"I'm coming out," he called. "My eyes are closed."

He walked toward her tentatively, listening to the sound the straps made in dragging up her arms to her shoulders, pulling the sheer triangles of fabric up over her breasts. Through hooded eyes, he watched her arrange herself.

"All right," she said.

He opened his eyes very wide. "I just got home," he said.

"What time is it?" she said.

He shrugged. "I stopped at a friend's," he said.

"What friend is that?" she said.

"Nobody," he said. "You wouldn't know him."

She leaned back onto the towel, crushing the rim of the hat. Eyes closed, she tipped her neck back, exposed her face to the sun.

"Benny out at the hives?" the boy said.

"Upstairs, I think," his mother said.

"Has he been out to the hives today?" he said.

"Who wants to know?" she said. "He'll probably go out with you, either way."

"If I want to go," the boy said.

"If you want to go," she said. She turned her head away. "Leave me alone a while," she said. 1: p144 • 1

He sat down on the hot cement next to her.

"What you been up to today?" he said.

"The usual," she said.

"You seen much of Benny?" he said.

"Same old, same old," she said.

"What has he been doing?" he said.

She locked her fingers behind her head. She pulled her head up to look at him.

"What little thing did I just ask of you?" she said. She let her head fall slowly back onto the towel. "Can't a woman tan?"

There were bees crawling about on the body and through the carpet and up the legs of the furniture. He went into the bathroom, opened the cabinet behind the mirror, took out a glass misty from water deposits and toothpaste spit. He dumped the toothbrushes out of it.

He carried the glass back into bedroom and began to fill it with bees. He took bees by their damp wings, lifting them up as their abdomens twitched, dropping them down into the glass. He opened the top drawer of the chest of drawers, fingered through underwear and medals and old Boy Scout awards until he found a plastic bag full of rings, traces of powder in it. He dumped the 2: p99 • 2 rings out into the drawer, turned the bag inside out, licked the powder off of it, slipped the bag down over the top of the glass.

He shook the glass until the bees were maddened. His mother was lying on her stomach, bikini top off again. He took the plastic bag off the glass.

"Get out of my sun," his mother said, without looking up.

He took a step back, put the plastic bag back on the glass.

"Where is a rubberband?" he said.

"Try the rubberband drawer," she said.

He went into the kitchen, opened the half-drawer, untangled a rubberband from the mess. He smoothed the bag down around the glass, putting the rubberband over the bag, staring at her out the kitchen window.

He took the shears from the knife block on the counter. He removed the latex gloves from their arthritic agony behind the faucet, shook them straight, slipped them on. They were warm and moist against his skin. He felt his hands already becoming slippery in them.

He climbed the stairs to the body, saw another bee crawling on the face. The bee made its way along the bridge of the nose and tucked itself down into the nostril, the end of its pulsing abdomen hanging out. He reached out, pinched his stepfather's nose shut, watched the bee's abdomen split and ooze yellow fluid.

His gloved fingers held the shears awkwardly. He opened the paired blades, sliding the bottom blade between his stepfather's lips, beneath the carpet thread. He cut through the thread, sheared off some of the lip with it. The opened flesh remained dull and bloodless.

Filling the mouth was a bolus of dead bees, squashed and stuck together, stingers missing. He poked at the clump, broke it apart, flicked smaller clusters of bee pieces out of the mouth and onto the carpet. The throat was crammed with bees as far down as he could reach, and farther.

He peeled the gloves off and left them bunched up, inside out, on his stepfather's bare chest. He moved the stiff jaw and pulled it wide open for the ceiling light to drive the shadows out of the mouth. He took a good, long look.

He looked at her naked back, his eyes tracing her spine up to the wide-brimmed hat hiding her face. He pulled the plastic bag off the jar slowly, watched the rubber band flip off and spin out over the cement. He leaned over his mother, shook the bees out onto her hat, watching them slide down along the rim.

"Whatever the hell you are doing, cut it out," his mother said, not moving.

He watched the bees wander over the pale, matted straw, watched each err its way through the vastness of that ridged expanse, test wings, vanish into the sky.

"No sign of Benny," the boy said.

"Hmm," she said.

"Any ideas?" he said.

"Try the bedroom," she said.

"I didn't see him," he said. He stuffed the plastic bag into the glass, set the glass down on the cement. "I'm going out to the hives," he said. "Coming?"

"No," she said.

"Come on, for a change," he said.

She sighed, stretched her fingers, her arms, her back. "Close your eyes," she said.

He did not close them.

1   He stood among the bees, spraying them with smoke. She kept her distance, leaning against the willow a few meters away, arms folded loosely over her bare stomach. He opened the hive and slid out a slat thick with honeycomb, aswarm with bees. He sprayed smoke over them until they fell off the slat, back into the hive. He felt the bees in his hair, on his hands, on his face.

"Know anything about bees?" the boy said to her.

She shrugged. She looked at him as if bored, then looked coldly away.

2: p26 · 2   He felt the sound of them all through him. He tasted the honey. He broke off a bit of honeycomb, cleaned the dead bees out of it, chewed on it.

3: p165 · 7   "What about sewing?" he said.

"I've done it before," she said.

"Clothes?" he said.

She shrugged. "Among other things," she said.

He held the rest of the honeycomb out to her.

She shook her head.

"Come over here," he said. "Mother."

He watched her bare feet leisurely picking their way back down the path, away from him, without hesitation. He lined up the grooves and slid the slat back in place. He sprayed himself with smoke, watched bees slow, stop, drop off.

She had taken the hat off, sticking it on the fencepost. The wind rocked it back and forth, ruffling the brim. The sun beat down on her back. Her eyes were closed.

"Benny's dead," he said.

She didn't say anything.

"Benny's dead," he said. "I mean it."

"Don't be tiresome," she said. "Just get the lotion."

He stood there a while, but then walked over and got the lotion from where it was by the glass doors. He carried it over, dropped the bottle onto the crease of her back.

"Rub it into me," she said. "Into my back."

He kneeled down beside her, opened the bottle, squeezed some out onto his fingers, began to rub it into her skin.

"Undo my top," she said. "Rub in circles, and evenly."

He fumbled her catch loose and pulled the straps off her shoulders and down her arms. He made long circular strokes until the white swirls of lotion vanished into her back.

"Good for a beginner," she said. "Don't neglect the sides."

He rubbed down the sides of his mother's body, feeling how the swelling edges of his mother's breasts were hot and dry under his lotion-slick fingers. He finished the back, remained hanging over her.

She stretched her bare arms far out in front of her. Ever so slowly she turned over. She tilted her head back.

"Now the front," she said.

He stayed there, on his knees, feeling the strength of his mother's small hands, pulling him, pulling him in.

Scene 27. Int. Morning.

<table>
<tr><td>1</td><td>This is a scene of mental preparedness in which Pierre rehearses his resolve to follow his mother's</td></tr>
<tr><td>2: p154 · 3</td><td>order: drink the infernal cup of debauchery to the very dregs or else... A scene marked by the</td></tr>
<tr><td>3: p162 · 1</td><td>double helix of shame and a terrifying hunger for pleasure. Although nothing happens on the</td></tr>
</table>

      This is a scene of mental preparedness in which Pierre rehearses his resolve to follow his mother's order: drink the infernal cup of debauchery to the very dregs or else... A scene marked by the double helix of shame and a terrifying hunger for pleasure. Although nothing happens on the diegetic level—Pierre sunk in his chair—this mental interlude is the essence of the imaginary register, rich and feverish with fantastic images assailing the young man as if he were a blank slate, a celluloid screen. *Il se fait son petit cinema.* The interior reverie starts with Rhea's striptease, which should be filmed all arms and legs, a slow liquid pan that loops back to the sluttish disorder Pierre encountered in his father's library. In this self-con game, Pierre tries to outwit the very thing that scares him to death by pretending to succumb to the most detailed phantasms his febrile imagination spits up. In accordance with libidinal economy's strange sense of time, he's cashing in on a pleasure check that hasn't been issued yet. It will be the director's challenge to evidence the splendid copula between film and desire.

CAMERA

Abiogenesis: a son will appear between those legs as meat left in the sun turns to maggots. A son will peer out from between those legs, a son who is all eye. A blink, a shudder of the legs. They fiddle together in silence. The son wants to cry. His lacrimal lake already full but crying implies a face. The son knows this, knows it in the way bivalves know food; not in the way the mother knows bivalves as food, as aphrodisiacs. She rubs the eye as she brings a bivalve to another orifice she can't see but knows is there. She knew it before the mirror confirmed its absence. An absence to slide bivalves down. The son, being rubbed, is negative light as rods and cones turn tactile. In the light there are shapes the son knows. He tears as pulses create the depths across which they travel. The son wants the shapes. The mother thinks back to lying on her back on a hillside covered in nondescript flowers. How the clouds inevitably became extant: sperm whales, their geysers too obvious. How naïve, she thinks, and drops another bivalve into the hole she can't see to celebrate her lost ingenuity. She can't see any of her holes. She cannot see the son. He cannot see her either, though her legs brace his field of vision. She stops rubbing for a moment, and the son opens to the world again; a subconjunctival hemorrhage lazily forming around his iris. What does he see, the mother wonders wrong-headedly. Eyes don't see. Minds see. The raw eggs arrive, and she goes back to rubbing, careful not to gouge the son in some imitation of an obvious act of creation. She sucks the eggs through pinpricks, sucking until the surface gives, and the yolk gushes like dirty sunlight into her. All the while a phenakistoscope persists along the surface retaining the son's aqueous fluid. The shapes more real to him than the shapes made by refracted light on photoreceptive cells in a manner consistent with their proper design.

1: p192 • 2

2: p172 • 1

1

The Forest of Clashing Erotics

SCENE

And here, at last, unless it is a dream, he sees his mother again, at once near to him and yet too far   *1*
away for him to hear what she is saying. Or is it simply that, seeing her again, he can hear nothing
through the blood beating in his ears?

But she is with another woman, the pair of them embracing and spinning each other about. Both
women elaborately masked, both wearing blousy white shirts, shirttails hanging down to cover
bare thighs, the tips of the tails parting and swaying with each step. Which is his mother again? All
he has by which to distinguish them are bare hands and the bare white skin stretching from knees
down tapering calves to steeply angled black pumps.

It is a gesture that gives her away. The woman on the left, talking animatedly to the other,
cocks her wrist oddly as if intending to scratch out the other's eyes. It is his mother's gesture, and
makes his heart leap in his throat. This must be his mother. But now the other mimics the gesture
and adds to it a slight and awkward ducking of the head. His mother's gesture as well. *This* must
be his mother then. But no, the curious way the first is now canting her hip, she must be…

So he is still standing at the hall's far end, watching and suffering, as the two women embrace,
pressing their masks against one another. He is longing to come closer but not daring, hoping that   *2: p161 • 1*
his mother will take pity on him, let him know which one of them she really is.

And of course she takes pity on him. She is his mother after all. Of course she eventually does.
The only problem: both of her do.   *3: p162 • 4*

And once he is thoroughly confused, once he is seeing his mother in two women at once, only then   *4*
do his two mothers seem to notice his presence. Only then does the fun really begin.

Scene 49. Int. Later that night. Inside Bains-Douches, nightclub.

1

2: p110 • 3

Without transition, we find Pierre in a sea of sweaty faces, pressing in on him, a collection of shadows, eyes, hair, shimmying to the thumping music, which he doesn't quite hear yet, in the dead of his own night, his own black fosse. When the heavy amplified sounds finally reach him, it's as if they have dragged him from under; his hand flies to his throat aware of a sudden ache there, a white patch in the strobe light. In between the dancing bodies, naked arches rolling this way and

3

4: p9 • 2

that, the flesh grows like a forest, snaking arms, cupped breasts, the long border of skin. Pierre lets the night have its way. Slow dissolve to a young dancer splashing her tresses onto him, whispering. Their conversation weaves in and out of earshot; what words can we imagine to draft this scene, to affix our initials on the dog-eared and yet always unlearned script of seduction? The veracity here can be shored up only by filming the scene as a question mark—the panic symmetry between

5: p220 • 2

night's beauty and unknowing is what brought our lead to the dance floor. The rest is nothing but referential sawdust under evening pumps.

New Orleans, June 18, 2005

Dear S.   *1: p50 • 3*

That sounds exactly right: church made out of what looks like nothing when sober.   *2*
Can understand the hallucinogenic, the sequencing of everything—talented dancers,
packed S&M.

That part that would have been self-consciousness was damaged. Watch and see how
men think. Close to home something bigger was coming. No excuse for the tension of   *3*
the possible storm.   *4: p189 • 3*

I miss you.

Love,
M.

Scene 32. Ext. Day.

1

Forward track following Pierre on the way to church. This is a silent, scabrous scene under the sign of mad laughter and convulsive self-consciousness. The more the young man laughs and chokes at the memory of Rhea's shameless words, the more he savors their turpitude, the more he craves to taste that wet shrine, the more he blesses her divine gift, and, face aflame, his entire body innervated by a strangling pleasure, he asks for death.

2: p157 • 5

3

4: p162 • 2

The camera moves from above to a darkened confessional: its lacy partition, shimmering shadows and rustling of priestly robes; a perfect vessel to convey Bataille's libidinal logic: the more unutterable, excessive and sacrilegious our pleasures, the more we cling to them. Outside, the sky darkens; lightning glares on a mangy dog eating his own vomit—overarching metaphor of man's subjection to his dark pleasures. Inside, eager to recite his sins, Pierre, like a delirious boxer, shifts his weight from one foot to the other as if wavering between defiance and remorse, all the while reveling in the temptation to not betray his mother. Now quite certain that he resembles her—like mother, like son—in vice and wickedness, he reels with happiness, knowing he'll walk to the end of the earth in her footsteps.

A few notes of a bar song hang at the cut.

PROPOSITION

That a proposition is not against any Law

that a moment of logic may be spurious

but logic

    for example:
        I see breasts that give milk
        They are real

             if the milk is not

who said that:

    (the point exactly of Law)

        the dialogue of one breast to another is
        surfeit

let all organs of logic be untamed   but let each lawful word modulate its organ

It would be possible to misunderstand "law" and "Law" and "logic"

1: p80 • 1   "   "

2: p105 • 1   *I do not want to explain it*

As far as one can know

3   the unearthly is not unearthly

so

4: 49 • 1   *the cause of a depression*

is the lake that fills it

fluid tonnage of logic

drink

proof   exit

in center   the lower case   the body   *1: p94 • 2*
leaning

toward it   this depression

I.e., in a slight misunderstanding   *make a site, then hollow it out*

reckless use of rules

calling   for example   memory a teat

(this recklessness acquired a body by cheating   *2: p164 • 3*

then demanded proof)

this was a mouth

(not the demand   *the proof)*

heretofore milk signified

belief

in nourishment

too much said and done   is
proof

make a mouth of it   jibing

Straighten your mockery

put a breast over a
blouse

1: p27 • 3   certain weather for the maternal

upends intention

whatever else was a breast for

but to obey

intention

as was always so
reckless

tamped down   utterly unbiased   impartial   depressed   logistically stable   erotic

Put a mouth over blouse between breast

and abeyance

rude with intention

That proposition

the point exactly of Law

lactates

naming for example

the mouth the organ who resided

on top of its garment

Labelling as such

the reckless ordering

is it

a propriety of truth

or thirst's obedience

dulce venenum, excès vénériens

romulus and remus erect statues of their mother, creating a sculpture garden filled with plaster   *1*
castings of her body. rhea sylvia as vestal virgin. rhea sylvia raped by mars. rhea sylvia birthing the
future of rome—twin boys, twin brothers molding their mother's body out of marble, travertine,
mortar. a body they've never known. their mother entombed alive after giving birth, her remains
shifting under dirt and the dust of buried relics. in their sculptures, she is always nude, and the
boys trail their hands over unfamiliar curves, over breasts never suckled, a womb once occupied,
now forgotten. their mother still a girl in their minds. in their monuments. the twins spend hours
amongst the sculptures, severing and rejoining limbs, posing her in every permutation. the horned-
rhea, the child-rhea, the saint. rhea the erotic—plaster hand between her legs, plaster head flung
back. placed in positions she could not possibly maintain. head bent between her legs, breasts
covering her belly, suckling herself—both she-wolf and foundling. they enter her as if she is a
virgin. breaching her hips in an inversion of birth—the two boys together, their sexes identical.
tongues pressed to the nipples, searching for milk. the boys finger the wet contours of her sex—so
smooth before the plaster dries—her nipples still pliable, her body damp and lithe. but the statues
always stiffen and sear, leaving the boys thirsting. their throats dry, their bodies parched for liquid.   *2*
the brothers moisten the materials. they manipulate the molds and recast the plaster. replicating
their mother's form until they have created a legion of rheas—a rome populated by her alone. the
boys grow old in their mother's company, spending days sitting before her, their heads resting on her
knees. at night, the boys dream of their mother, and in their dreams, she is dreaming of them. her   *3: p165 • 3*
muscles flexing under her skin. each movement decadent. as she prowls the garden. her sculptures   *4: p14 • 1*
spread across acres. thousands of rheas recumbent. amassed like an army at the city gates.

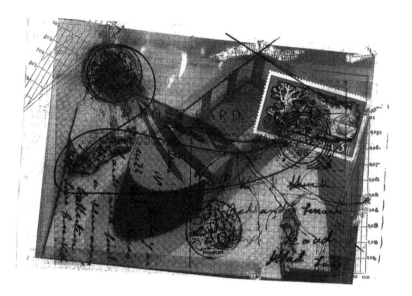

1: p155 • 1

DISCRETIONARY (VIRTUAL)

the house she occupies perfect without her   *1*
her copy of I Capture the Castle among bits of Lego

I will never surrender the castle,
the rambling splendor of Sleaze

She-ra Kay Princess of Power. A Kitten's Prayer.=^..^=

I've trapped her
legs, she's tucked in tight. Here I pass the night.
I am
'Queen'   *2: p151 • 3*

She and Princess play for hours. When she got back she was horribly
abused. She stood at the shower opening
closing curtains when the princess bathed
she was a princess and would like to get warm
kittens don't get wet   drowned
with their tongues, clean
tongues are muscles
what do tongues mime?
"We shall see if she's a princess," thought the queen without uttering a   *3: p172 • 7*
word
posturing
descriptions and bookmarks

professional
confessional rights produce
cosplay
sodaplay: home of creative play.
usurp syrup sugar

QUEENIE

1   My name began with cookies.

Shortbread pinwheels sandwiched with lemon filling.

I stuffed the pinwheels into my coat pockets at the end of my shift at Teak's. Six pinwheels per pocket. There are some things you don't get tired of.

We weren't supposed to take whole cookies, and especially not the pinwheels. Peter the boss said they used real lemon zest and zest doesn't come cheap. He kept a cleaned-out paint tub with cookie duds in the break room. Duds are broken, cracked, misshapen, or unfilled cookies. The three old Greek women brought plastic sacks to work and filled them with duds. I can't eat pinwheels broken and rubbed up with other broken cookies.

"The cookies end up mixed together anyway," the old Greek women say, "plop, brown cookie torpedoes," they snicker and bring their long white hair to their faces like veils.

Peter caught me with my pockets full one day.

He pulled me by the collar into his office, keeping me close like he had a gun. A river smell to Peter, green water and rope.

2: p67 • 4

3   Peter's office was lit by small gold restaurant lamps with red fringe. The lamps matched the Persian rug Peter bought at the Alladdin close-out sale. The world is meaner, the old Greek women say, without the Alladdin's kibi and butter beans with chili mango pickle.

"Empty them," Peter said, gun finger pointing at my pockets.

"But they'll break," I said in a little girl voice, innocence worth a try. If I hadn't been late that morning my hair would have been in braids which I could have swung behind me.

"That's the whole point," Peter said, "get it? The *whole* point?" Hands now on hips, Wranglers 28W, dark brown with leather trim.

I turned my purple satin coat pockets inside out and let the pinwheels fall. Out came the condom I stole from the men's bathroom. The kicked-in machine gives you condoms without paying so we all have sex more.

"Well, what do you know," Peter said, "another infraction," and bent down for the condom slim as a stick. He stepped on a pinwheel that hadn't broken, the pinwheel snapping loud beneath the tip of his tan snakeskin boot like it was plastic.

"Drop the coat, too," he said and I let it fall. The coat from the Hasbeen thrift store, bought because of the deep pockets. Purple plaid wool that's not really my style. Jim Hasbeen insisted the purple made me look wan and Victorian.

Peter set the condom on a long wood dining table piled with papers. Papers held down by geodes from his camping trips. Some girls leave his office with geodes in their fists. They display them afterwards face out in their work cubbies. Pink, blue, white, ivory or violet crystals inside ordinary brown rock. Some girls have more than one.

"Their hooties are same as pretty rock hooties," the old Greek women say, wagging their wet tongues so their spit falls on the floor.

My hootie, though I prefer puss, is ordinary brown.

I held out my arms, not all the way but halfway to let Peter know I was ready for the pat-down. Hootie girls say his pat-downs are better than anything their boyfriends do. No boy has spent much time on me. Get in and get out.

My heart beat the way that it does around Hush. Just being close to sex.

Hannah said Peter touched her boobs for like an hour. He won't do that with me. Flat mounds that never rose. All because I didn't do the chest exercises Mom swears gave her a D cup. Not even wearing a bra today. Boys like the surprise of that. Like seeing themselves but smoother.

"Okay, now let me check you out," Peter said. No question he was looking at my nipples that weren't hidden by pockets, worn especially for Hush. "Arms up for a minute," he said, "might be cookies under your shirt."

Hurt to raise my arms, lifting boxes of shortening and sacks of flour all week. A sweat smell to me but also the perfume from Daria's purse, musk and melon, sure to capture Hush.

Peter opened and closed his hands like counting to one hundred and then cracked each knuckle.

I stepped towards him, make the reach shorter, suspense in my throat.

He warmed his hands in front of the electric heater under the table, red coiled and crackling like a campfire.

"Lower the arms," he said, and I lowered them slow like being at the doctor's. The pat-down will make me well. My breath came out like blood or spit, anything fluid we can't stop.

His hands went first to my face, the pads of his fingers warm. He drew a slow trail—hard to explain, those girls said, and now I know—trailing over my neck, shoulders, back, my muscles resting under his touch like a hot bath and the whole time he's breathing full like he's outdoors on one of his hikes.

I closed my eyes and watched wildflowers in Hen canyon. The wildflowers Dad showed me the week before he died. Red, yellow, and purple flowers. Wind jiggling thin petals and stems, hardier than you think. Hen canyon named after a golden beak of rock.

Peter finished his trail at my ankles. Every part of me sang, hot and eerie. Didn't take an hour but I can say it did.

"You can take the pinwheelies now," Peter said, and pointed to the floor. His johnnie strained the cloth of his pants, skinny like an English cucumber not all the way grown. He handed me a lunch bag, shook it to shoo my eyes off his pants, an apple still in the bag. Peter's mom packs his breakfast and lunch. Every morning, two sacks. B and M. Lots of jokes about that.

1

2: p98 • 3

3

4: p49 • 3

5: p195 • 11

6

1   "No one eats the apples," I said, and rolled the apple out of the sack.

Peter kicked the apple but missed. "She means well," he said.

I went down on my hands and knees and picked up the pinwheels. Lucky for me I inherited a round ass like Dad. He showed it off too. Tight seats Mom had to mend.

Cold floorboards the heater didn't reach and dirt from Peter's hiking boots, little brown V's I had to ditch. The pat-down song wearing off.

2   My ass covered in red stretchy velvet. McQueen pants that took months to buy on layaway from Shores department store. Red velvet too good for work but the pants fit me like the skin of an apple. I wore them for Hush, who ended up switching shifts to be with Hannah.

"Looks like you need some help down there," Peter said, and he got on all fours himself. "Cute little zipper," he said, "a teardrop," and unzipped the back of my pants slowly, another trail, giving me time to say stop.

Sound of the zipper, the metal teeth parting, the teardrop at the base of my ass. I don't have to do this but I do.

Hannah on TV one on the upper wall of the office. Doing what I'd just left off doing. Squirting eyes on cupcakes. Frosted turkeys on pumpkin cupcakes for Thanksgiving, hundreds of them. Hush on TV one, too. Bent over Hannah while she squirted.

"McQueen?" Peter said, the label in my pants stitched in gold thread on black, a crown with a tiny bunny beside it. Peter, called Eagle-Eyes by the owner of Teak's. The owner gave him a real eagle he shot by accident. Had it stuffed on the QT by the guy who fills the holiday breads, crushed walnuts with orange and rosewater.

Peter peeled off my McQueen's.

"So white, your skin," he said, and blew on my ass like I'd powdered it.

My white skin came out of nowhere, Mom said. Everyone else ruddy.

Peter unbuckled his too long for him belt, a second prick the girls say.

The old Greek women laughed on TV two as if they could see us, their mouths black.

"Would you hand me that?" Peter said, meaning the condom on the table, and I reached for it, stretching my torso lean, no fat in my waist like Hannah. "You ever see Steve McQueen in *Bullitt*?" Peter said, fiddling with the condom, not what I thought he'd say but I'm all for casual. He felt for my puss like he couldn't see, didn't want to get the wrong place.

He pushed his johnnie into me while the youngest old Greek woman shimmied her loose boobs in her greek gown.

3: p10 • 7   I needed the fuck.

4: p87 • 2   Wet all week imagining me and Hush in the broom closet. All those handles and Hush so large.

A field trip of kids on the TV three. The woman teacher looking through the hole of a wedding ring cookie at the man teacher with her, the man teacher already married. That glued and can't get unstuck look to him.

Peter fucked me in time with the stamper on TV four, *bee-ta, bee-ta, bam, bee-ta, bee-ta, bam,* pinwheel crumbs digging into my hands and Peter's legs sweating, kind of icky but the taken-over feeling of being fucked worth a million crumbs. Hannah not on TV one, just Hush smoothing his hands together, a nervous habit.

Bee-ta, bee-ta, bam, and Peter stopped, threw his body over mine like a log on a campfire and came.

The old Greek women as if they could see us, their black-hole eyes, the oldest wiping spit off her chin.

"Damn hags," Peter said, and rolled his body off mine. He grabbed a box of cotton gloves, the closest thing, and mopped up. "Here, let me give you a hand," he said and laughed, what he's done and said before.

I mopped up while Peter swept the rest of the broken pinwheels under the table, the janitor his brother.

Peter gave me a geode with ivory crystals that looked like teeth. No cubby geode has teeth. He also gave me four packages of mint marvels—the most expensive cookie, real mint and real Swiss chocolate. Mint marvels for my suitcase, emergency food to go with my emergency clothes. I'm prepared to leave at any time, I tell Mom.

The next day at Teak's I stuffed the pockets of my purple plaid Victorian coat with pinwheels and the same thing happened.

When Peter held my hips that time he called me Queenie.

Queenie.

Peter wanted to name a new cookie *queens*. Shortbread filled with raspberry cream and dipped in dark Belgian chocolate. *Kings* is what they ended up being called, after the owner's dog. Peter later got fired for pulling the wrong kind of girl into his office. A virgin, the old Greek women say.

If that virgin hadn't squealed, those cookies would be named after me.

1: p81 • 2

2: p75 • 5

3

4: p136 • 1

[16th & Mission]

BART ii. head bandage replete with hole

[loose change on cigarette scarred park bench]

1: p209 • 2   she is tagged at the wrist
2: p49 • 1   a suitcase on a passenger plane
left hand drawn up
in the universal sign of
i have a headache

she balances without
effort

Dear Kelly,

This winter, everyone's hunched over in their own private airplane seats, sight-reading the street. Do I deserve new clothes? Ugh, what a repetitive gesture. They say you've also "parted ways" with your 2002 image. If you look on IMDB you'll see some people like your ass but not your face. This puts me in such a despondency I know now how I want the book to end: on a crease.

1: p198 • 8

2: p40 • 2

3: p93 • 3

2 4

"It's getting colder," she said.

"Let me show you something."

The two of them walked behind the house and stood on the edge of a long gravel driveway.

1: p59 • 1 There was nothing to look at, just the dark disappearing behind the trees. Back at the house, light was framed in the window.

As Caroline walked home, two people were lighting the lights along a road.

It was the blind man and another man, but they were on a different road than she was.

2: p57 • 3 Caroline began to read *The Fold*.

Josephine walked into the cabin, stamping her feet on the rug to knock the mud loose from her hiking boots.

"Hi."

"Hi."

"I was making the rounds."

3: p93 • 2 "I'm reading *The Fold*."

4 Josephine poured hot water into a cup. "Are you thirsty?"

5: p101 • 2 Caroline walked to the window of the cabin and opened it.

"What do you hear?"

6: p62 • 3 Caroline listened but it was hard to hear anything. She could only hear what was happening inside the cabin. Like Josephine crossing the room and laying something on the desk. She listened to those sounds for a while.

7: p165 • 2 "Do men like you as much as they did when you had two hands?" Caroline asked.

"No," Josephine said.

"Do you have a boyfriend?"

Dear Kelly,

At a cold blue table a horn pinches at the air, its leads, its gestures. I didn't
want to depart from the recording but my lungs had started to feel the
effects of television's unfinished repair. Like my sister's face on the flute,
that greenery, suburban pointillism, I'm not even sure you can read music.
I am so tired of pointing, just pointing.

1

[Mission & 19th]

mission st. & 19th st with grey gardens

she wore three scarves
edie did on her head water
pistol poised

'database.   database! '

'it rhymes with reality.
not wishfulness or pandering.'

[Geary & Larkin]

because it was shapeless
over there in the dark
we sat two
          to a seat
and sipped sweetly on straws
until the fifth one came
              tipping neatly into a two
breaking the rhythm completely

                              here is where alien
                              comes into play

moleskin notebooks
scraps of pieces and papers
your skull cap my stack of
          red straws
me sitting a fingertip away

                              here is where the boys
                              come in

to play blonde haired bob   1: p50 • 3
secured with a clip,
tip sparkles
against the rhythmic purple
light in the jukebox
          I swear you say
you too but I think no
              the organ
it's all swimming in my head   2: p10 • 2
sometimes I think of you
because I am dizzy   3: p57 • 1

here is where the hip swinging
poke poke

of a finger we
were into play sitting
two by two again
        blondie was off-off
he said yes
Japanese, Korean, Vietnamese
        definitely Asian

here is where we drove

Geary
a blur I don't remember
        looking
alien— he said
1, 2, 3, 4

counting as in them
then I remembered
        the capital A

Dear Kelly,

I hear you've parted your hair a new way for the music video. I myself
am dividing tasks according to what can be completed in front of the
television, the depressive's gesticulations toward order. On my complaint   *1*
letter to the airlines, my "sincerely" has been upgraded to "best wishes"
— the twitching rabbit of ordinary brutality. Small bones, you say. Still,   *2: p3 • 1*
you must protect your throat from the hawks that can swoop down like the   *3*
next big lie.   *4: p65 • 1*

DISCRETIONARY (PAPER)

=^..^=

flower frog
1: p14 • 1 garden lovers club
Flower Divider. Purple Flower Blooming EVALUATION

chance to be   friends
a spell on her   would be like
Screamin' Jay Hawkins

                            grew up with
go out for drinks with friends and talk about men
                    inventive ideas for crazy

2: p39 • 4 a woman authors her own life, exerts, initiates,
                    "I want that"   she would say if could say   boy toy
3: p63 • 1 uses her friends as fill-ins between relationships
4: p103 • 4 She's making the car trip in memory
                    Do you have a car?   sales opportunity
long hours on transport   gadgets kill time
Do you have the accessories you need?   sales opportunity

only she reclaims the word
not a closed system, one where rhetoric
I was surprised to hear from her
                    expression   duplicity
                                        duplication
                                        twinning 2

OUR FATHERS

I.

My mother called to say Rebecca's father passed away. When we were in high school, I saw Rebecca's father come and go. Rebecca's mother divorced her father when Rebecca was a baby.

II.

When we were teens, Rebecca's father would order us to get him things when he was over at Rebecca's. He'd tell us to get him beer, and open it, put it right there on the table. He had a deep and smoky voice. I would sit in Rebecca's living room, staring at her father. Rebecca would talk to her father about things like the suntan she was getting, and she would readjust her strap to show her tan line.

1: p18 • 3

Sometimes, when I stayed overnight in Rebecca's double bed, I would get up and get a drink of water. Her father would be sleeping on the sofa. Sometimes I liked to watch him.

III.

When Rebecca met my father, he still lived on the farm where I grew up, and we stayed there for a weekend. He was outside most of the duration, in the fields, plowing them and planting.

Rebecca and I lay in the backyard, trying to get sunburned. My parents built that house when I was eleven. After they built the house, my mother got a job and then my father had a breakdown, and the next year, my mother left my father.

2: p152 • 3

My father passed us in the yard. We wore bikinis. He stopped and looked at us and smiled. We looked up, shading our eyes with all our fingers. He smiled again. Rebecca smiled back. She told me he was cool and that she liked him.

3

IV.

1

2: p195 • 5

Rebecca married a guy she dated back in high school. I remember the picture of her in her wedding dress, smiling with her father, his arm around her. There was one with him hugging her, his white moustache pressed against her bridal collar. I got married at a courthouse. My marriage lasted for a year.

V.

When we were in church, my father yelled in the middle of the sermon, "God help me, help me, help me. Our Father Who Art in Heaven, God help me, help me, help me."

VI.

3

I went to see my father at the institution. I had to get directions. I stopped at a gas station and bought a map.

The nurse handed me to someone, who took me to his room.

"Who are you," he said.

"I'm your daughter, Dad." I looked at the checkers game he had been playing. I asked him if he wanted to play checkers.

4

He smiled then. He sat in a chair. He had held me once when I was younger. I'd seen it in a picture.

VII.

For Independence Day, I'd gone to Rebecca's father's cabin for the weekend. We all sat in the sun, and later we went rafting. Rebecca played in the sand with her two children, and her father sat with me. We reclined, laying on our lawn chairs. We talked about the ocean. He was retired. He smiled at me. I let him.

2 9

image of glass on the wall between doors, which is outside the stream of thought (being) present
the moment she answers the phone, person the father calls the next morning knowing she is awake   *1*
in the painting (unconscious) the first of whose figures appears to be thinking "I am dreaming"

feeling that way about such a person (intuitive) as kneeling down beside her in a form of thought,
object present in the sense that she can touch him or look at the picture a second time, watercolor
the daughter paints driving along the coast to meet someone (conjecture) under certain circumstances   *2*

motion of trees against a blue sky, white rose on the neighbor's wall not in focus at that distance   *3: p112 • 8*
possibly literal, as a woman walking in from the left isn't expected (deviation), glimpse of bird
in a straight line (emphasis) as the man leans into a curve below which slate of current moving   *4: p66 • 1*

1: p52 • 4

PHOTOGRAPH IN WHICH EVERYTHING IS BLURRED

2

Muscled in sun. The song of the lark: a girl with a scythe, mouth agape (a gap) as listening as singing. Meaning to pour

liquid from a bottle down one's throat without touching one's lips so one cannot help but think of kissing as in novels the only

3: p199 • 1
4: p212 • 2

kiss is to say so and so kisses so and. (I always heard O'Hara was killed by a dune buggy; it was a Jeep.)

Dear X,

A man keeps bumping into the same woman—over a three-month period—in different locations. The man and the woman exchange hellos and how-are-you's. They smile and become silent. The man, nervous to continue talking, and avoiding the silence, wonders if he should say: "We meet so often, under such strange circumstances, maybe we should begin having sex." He doesn't say anything, though, and then she and he say goodbye.

1: p1 • 4

2: p204 • 1

dear jack,

you're so full of shit. best we get that out of the way earely. the stereo is on and as bob said "they got so much things to say right now". and you and you and yuou.

saturday night jack, it was warm until said she come in. "inner realm". she actually said that. saturday night jack, I like that. you're "saturday night jack" now you fucker.

1: p45 • 1   said I was lucky to be there while she removed her ugly face.

2   "when was the last time you kissed on someone"

"when I was thirteen"

"no really"

3: p18 • 1   thirteen was a black-out jack. the color on me changing. blush. I wouldn't mind if a girl wanted to be a guy. wouldn't mind it all being on my shoulders. wouldn't mind driving all night. wouldn't mind if it was only whatever it was she wanted. as long I get to darken my shade.

"were not going to start asking questions like that are we"

"maybe not"

you may think I was being funny but she had a hideous face. it was like someone left some clay
4: p75 • 3   in the sun too long and it cracked. years of cocaine and bennies and cooking up those little spponoons. little sppooonnnsss.

so it wasn't a surprise when she took off all six feet of herself. all sex fett of her. me all naked myself. wait, let me go back.

me through you jack on the way to her house I stoppped thinking, stopped receiving if you will because I had decided I would. I imagined her putting her hand next to my skin just to feel my heat. but that was the qustion. shade.

"let's meet for coffee"

"why don't I just come over your place"

and she was easy for that. me thinking I'd drive all night just to be late. hten I was there. soon as I'm in the door,

"let's go out somewhere"

"do we have to"

"are you ashamed to be seen with me"

"no, I just thought it might be interesting to see what's in the other room" and I'm already so tired of the weight of you. the wait of you. the stare me down. avoiding myself for days at a time, but not for any of the good reasons. just trying to get through the day without losing my shit. and then I thought of the girl in the red dress from the night before. because you start thinking of people sometimes just to stop. you think of them and then you know and they they appear in front of you with their boyfriends and they and him, god, well he was so nice jack. my btetter nature then. my happiness spread around the room. violins. singers drowned in the swell.

1

me all naked myself. feigning some interest and then turning out the light. thinking about the night before and that I finally met a girl named maggie. maggie a friend of the girl in the red dress. so I thought of them both. al;ll this distraction jack to say that I used her. she had an ugly face and a beautiful body. fuck the body to get past the face. cancel me from the unadvantagetakers.

2: p43 • 2

so after we finished the phone rings in that place where you wake. or she wakes with an idea in her head that was in my head or on page 24 in a book I was reading thatt day. either way, we wake not knowing where we are. I'm a middle of the nigh t man but yuou know that. I was young for a minute or two. like I could write on the air. or tell it in some ear. but it didn't last long. we were figuring it out. we were done and the condom was in the trash. we were starting to tell lies.

3: p178 • 7

"are you sure"

"it was great"

"just that"

"it's better than doing it for myself"

"that what you've been doing"

"for about eight months"

then her father on the answering machine aand the piano off somewhere in the left side of my head. my hand next to her ugly cheek while she listened. blood rising. the window cracked in her bedroom. the front door unlocked. still in her. dogs barking. all the good people. so many of them. something seeps in then. as if maybe the two of you could be two people who long to be awkward.

4: p53 • 1

"I thought it was this guy"

"whichy guy"

"this guy who called me at work one day"

"for what"

"a survery, but he had this cool accent, brithish, and when he was done he siad could he do antying for me and I said you can tell me your name and pretty soon he's talking to me. he's saying things I'd never thought of"

me in bed jack thinking our time has passed so quickkly.

"so what happened"
"I gave him my home number and he starts calling. and every night it go hotter if that's possible. I'd take out my magic wand and he'd talk and it just got better and betterh"
"magic wand"
"it's in a drawer there next to the bed"
"wherewas he calling from"
"modesto"
"whatwas his name"
"that was part of the rules, no names. I don't even have his number, he always called. and then one night he didn't. two months go by and he didn't call."

that small truck of mine jack. you waking me up every morning on the trip down east. heads swimming a sun rize over the atlantic. west then to find our own big easy. that squid in the aquarium impenetrable. I kept starring until your reflection in the glass felt like a relieft. you can get get under the water of yourself. do an impression of release. "this is my friend jack, he's the mayor of new orleans".

three days rideing that italian trolley girl out to tulane. you and you and yuou and her into each others eyes like there was something to see. I was derelict with her first saturday night, I'll bett you don't even remember that.

how long can someone be not yours, knot touched and nothing more before she stays that way.

"what time is she coming home"
"she's probably home now. I need to use your shower"
"god, my showers so dirty, I'll have to clean it"
"don't, I just need to stopp smelling like what we just did"

I hated you the most in arizona jack. you didn't know that. two days direct to california through the nihgt and the night to wash off new orleans. it's like seeing something through a film. an ugly girl in clean sheets.

I need to take some time off now to resist myelf. back in a half hour. while I'm gone you can pretend you see everything coming. think about the fact that girls always seem to kiss girls before I meet them. never after. or that car that cut me off in west texas when you were sleeping.

yeah, I'm back and I'm thinking where do I find it. in women I guess. at the same time remembering page 24. I can't get over certain ideas once I read them. something about the way we pass through. as if we were singular. it never occurred to me that way before. how easily we're passing through all this darkness just out of our sight. and her in that red dress smiling like *1: p98 • 1* it was her birthday.

I locked the door and ran the bath at her house. she was right, the bathtub needed cleaning. *2*
I traced designs in the bath water with my finger. almost two in the morning maybe. the schedule of taking pills. open up, swallow. drop one on the floor for the sound. flick one at the wall. let one *3: p104 • 3* slip into the bathwater with you. another for the open window. give one to a homeless man. take extra for a wide clearing. money changing hands. no one wants to part with the let go they allow. goingpast movingpast, days move by like hours. join the ranks. poppers. we who need some skin in our lives.

I just felt some static when I touched the back of my neck. *4*
IU miss you jack,
grady *5: p9 • 2*

Dear all mouses,

I caution you to stay at home, for men are much like lions in Ohio. Men like sleeping cats in grass.

From Ohio, one in New York might clarify, lick great paw and tell of leaving such a place—not on a hunt—although prey happens—but on a quest for quarries dried of water.

Dearest mouses, know this: In this world we have the offered and the asked for.

Lions, those from Cleveland, tend to send grant applications for the stone to come to them. Half-faced by grass, this one I'll use as an example pants and wonders why the wait. He's planned for nothing but to get the quarry, place his body on the highest rock, reach a certain height then fall to sleeping in the latter-day sunlight. In his broadened nose, his growl-full yawn, one could find a way to want this lion who wants this quarry—a mouse who skitters by his feet as he goes *walk walk walk* away, on deadened grass—as he gives in, and goes in search for stone on which to lie.

1: p39 • 1

There is the offered, dearest mouses. There is the searched for.

2: p205 • 2

A stone on which to say he's made it somewhere.

Our mouses hearts beat two bazillion every time we skit away from stomping paws. But *oh*, we mouses think. But *oh*, the lion's paw.

—Yours in solidarity, K

Dear Kelly,

I feel it's time to wear more skirts, it's time to change brains, it's time to up my dose, it's time for less empathy. I don't have any appetite for this appetite. I tell my lover she's my little Hamlet when she cries and cries.

1: p10 • 7
2: p104 • 3

Let me explain: the feeling there's something else you're supposed to be doing is terrible as a flock of birds. I tried to up the antecedent. I was fit to burst with words. Honey, I wanted the hit.

3

Lover,

1

2: p112 · 4

3

4: p44 · 4

The smallest slants keep happening today. All day. It's the loosening of eye teeth. Tastes intrude like how the classical can weave it. The moment more real. Snap of your head when you thought you heard something move in the foyer. Here, drawing shutters, nearing midnight, simultaneously you're there, the morning train towards sea, sitting backwards. Newsprint on your teacup.

Liver,
Even

New Orleans, July 6, 2005

Dear S.

A different regret every night—and afterwards. Just the time getting past. I listen to the men and she talks. Together, we are a whole person. Alone, I am a cold, flat. I can see why they mind.

1: p1 • 5

Surreptitious faking. Muddy because everyone uses. So many possible loves flickering. Each one wants to weave his own pattern into the rug.

2: p105 • 3

But how can I practice this Southern Belle thing without you?

Love,
M.

Meanwhile,

1

Here I am in domestic bliss and blister. Sleep spurs tangles. I took
a pair of perfectly, but they were yours. She threatened suicide
2: p22 • 5 the evenings I did not. It's already inside you, and submission.
Collections I hope to keep discretely. This year's little sense. Your
commentary: A twinned sigh across the airshaft. Dry crackle the
3: p112 • 7 blues. Soft metal. Buckled love.

Mine

Dear U,

It has occurred to K that everyone may be dead, and this is what is after life—a small   *1*
occasion near a sea or wheatfield, a joke that pokes under a layering of disguises, that   *2*
vestigial sense of being incomplete in the hours alone. But how does one know if the
next person is a false friend, a vampire, or an installation from a dream, partly observed?
Why is there water?   *3: p156 • 4*

RIVER

1: p195 • 6

The birds walked out, open beaked

on water

to stand   for everything

2: p84 • 1

like a river

and slow megaphone of sound on water

3: p156 • 4

and footprint of water

a gather

of my electric form

PAT WALLECK'S LEG

I won it in a poker game, his leg,   1

the first prosthesis a cross   2

between grasshopper and trombone,

scraped up from when his girlfriend

shoved him down the long steel stairs.   3: p47 • 3

We never talked him into the Walnut River   4

where minnows nibbled our hair,

our bench a submerged upriver elm.

Instead he tossed us beers from the bank,   5: p143 • 1

and menthol cigarettes in Ziploc.

Fake leg unstrapped from stump,

he could have leapt in head first,

and swam. But would not. He died   6

at twenty-eight. I avoided him at the end.

When his leukemia came yawning

out of hibernation, I made my clumsy

pilgrimage to the shrine of St. Roch

on St. Roch Street, surrendered my prize

to the room where other hopers had left

braces, trusses, videotaped mastectomies,

plaster casts of hands feet elbows faces.

Pat's leg made the shrine a leg show

for an audience of unblinking Jesus

and St. Lucy's eyes on a platter.

Do your work, I asked the statues, not seeing how.   7: p16 • 7

In the best elegy for my friend,   8

which this can't be, he'd be left high

on the riverbank watching us

across the slow water. Back then he knew

more than we could fool ourselves about. Let alone now.

MERCENARY BEVERAGES

4:30 a.m.
last 3 fools ali-
ing (ozzy playing?
How?) w/ gob
let of French
coffee pot
bottom fed
w/ remaining
1: p198 • 6   4.5 beers of
mixed breeds.
"The glories
of miscegenation!"*
Let's get Pagan!
& blo up the back
2: p112 • 8   of the yard
w/ fire crack
ers. We must needs
cigarettes 4 punks.
Next day, epiphany-
proof vests shed
off: aspetta! we're
not trash — panda &
bouquet of relict
bottle rocket chop
sticks from Heine
kens !

* F.S.

Noonish
3 cripples pool   3: p67 • 2
ing (where's da
p.t.) w/ chlor
inated H2 0
everywhere none
to drink (privit
ized) shorts no
pot but more per   4: p99 • 3
haps social, but
the gories of
social segregation
Forget Reagan?
& blow up the knows
of the craft
with air booty
"unhip hop." Need
on the vicadin just   5: p59 • 2
can't wait to get on
the bike again, after
noon-proof clocks
go cop-poof, yet proof
of flower law flour
power hour followers
oh yeah, the journey
man   6: p98 • 5

PULL YOUR EARS BACK

"...to me it's putting an equal sign between the opressed and the oppressor; 'it's all the same' and that's why it's so problematic. Because there is no equal sign between the defensive violence of the oppressed and the aggressive violence of the oppressor. One has nothing to do with the other."

—*Joyce Chediac*

As the warring words in the 45 flipside of scratched Fuchxtique throat bomb once spoke; "got a wall at vic making taggz into music/aerosol as needles/strikes can become addictive/hittin bricks with wacks."

Pull yuh ears back and come see where we left off... I once saw a guy on a bus once stab himself in the kneck. I guess it didn't phase him none cuz he did it again 5 more times. He lived. Perminant nerve damage, though — lives life on a tilt. His name was Assassin. He had held his protest to demonstrate the loss of his son to his woman. His star's name = Hakim.

Assassin considered his star a little blessing. You can't get phet wrong. Hakim, he his likkle man. He is his special/special. Same as thought Løcel. For every person there is a driver and a witness. Assassin had hooked onto the meds they piled him with for the twisted pain of his tilt. His disability checks kinda wore him out cuz they felt he could, and he wanted to, but nadabody would hire him and his sad/sads made him mad/mean and so he grew farther from seeing his star cuz the wisdom said so — the ministry made it so, cuz they said so, and so his wisdom became their wifey and naw he felt he had no life.

So Assassin started walking around with a compressed copy of the New Testament in his breast pocket and took to watching feggits give head in parks to Gay Cop Bob.

He'd sit off on tree hump and crank some criz and yai till he spunked and cried at the thought of the possibility of feggitry and world gone crazy.

I wanna make you feel the pain that I experience.

Bus rides and suicide — attempted recovery and reviews for disability.

H8's daddy had heart stoppage one day when he got into a shout off with a worker who had to take the loser cruiser cuz their car was in the shop. That was the

1: p175 • 1

2: p10 • 1

same worker who had cut him off just after last xmas. He wanted to know where his star was. He wanted to let the mofo know that he had worked all his life. That he had pulled his welly fam through food banks at the St Vince de Paul and family shelters and worked at pizza joints and garages since he was 16… dealt with feggit cokeheads and wolves. He saw his lil cousin walk around in phat gear and a ball cap with a big "P" on it and a bitch by his side. He hear about him later got setup inna apt by two crackers who claimed to be scrappin over the betty and they clipt him in the head and lil cuz never woke up from a premamant daydream, woh. Assassin had been avoiding giving jobs $\{\pi\}$ but had been working every job imaginable = ol buildings, tearin, painting, dry wallin, lifting rocks and slangin math, attending Aryan meetings, chompin on pain killers and chuggin cheap whiskey, pretending to be a str8 up cracker, in hopes for an everlasting handout in this new construction colonial + unskilled workers = the big product;

-Am i My slavERY, MUFFAFOOKCA?!!!. My struggle-

pphhzzzzt!

…and now he got a star of his own — a lil boy — he call him Hakim — Listen to Assassin's heart sing;

Coo yah. Coo yah. Look there.

Hey yaeh

My lil boy he can jump

he can run/he can run

he can jump/he can run

he can run

he can jump

Coo yah. Coo yah

Hey yaeh

yo

Watché la.

he can jump/he can run

he can run

…

Coo yah

My lil boy

Hey yaeh

yo

he can jump

he can run

he can jump

he can run

he can jump

he can run

he can jump

he can run

he my lil one

…and they take him and call Asssassin lazy? Get a job? He a bum? Junkie fookcah? Get to work? Yuh friggin cock suckah? His striking of his days for his ismah.

-I LIVE LIFE ONNA TILT, MUFFAFOOKCA!!! KNOWLEDGE PHET!!!-

So he had issues. …and this lil wigga at the food bank, day before last, was hassling him for 60¢ for a likkle fake point of uppertunity that he had alledged to have fronted him. He waited every lunch hour on the lawn inna ramble of garbage bags, sleeping bags and karate kicking prison toned grads who had made it from the juvi to the pensive state higher learning institutes — tummies as tight as a ripple chip practicing the fußball kicks — aiming their strikes at the street corner cams, they would knock out for the common wealth, while hoping to hook up or peddle their trade with a bwai pimp who went by the name of Jimmy the K. It was Jummy the K who walked around with a pimp cup, woht he got at a micky ds, which he had glued shellacked gummy bears, polished glass, bamma rubies and latino figurines he all got from the gumball machines at the mall.

…and it was Jimmy the K woht was giving Assassin hassles for the .60¢. Jimmy the K approached him as Assassin did his dance wave, bending his ankles side to sway, dipping his hands into his empty pockets for change that was long gone, since last xmas, and swept My tar with his peepers, and the edges of the sidewalk beneath him, for a dropped fatty butt to roll a slut with.

1: p218 • 4

pphhzzzzt!

…and he said 'where's my money b@tch' or something like that woht you're suppose to say from a downloaded skit and he cackled something bout Assassin being a 'rip off artist' or something and Assassin said this and that and that he didn't 'owe him shit' after sayin "woh" or something and questioned the entire integrity if the issue and the credibility of the dastardly wigger — which Jimmy the K felt that he had to now defend, and all that street cred sitiation, which seemed a lot more important than what a media hooper would give a fookc about on any given channel or press.

So was it time to swang? a woh/woh? Woht time was it? was it time for a knuckle up? awo, wanna juggle, wigga? too early to handle your liquar?

-muffafookca-

b.u.t. nada, the chins kept their wiggle and the hands remained untransformed

1: p167 • 2

into knuckles and the crowd never really gathered and the street reverands never came out to settle. All woht got done was a crizkid, who use to be a sk8er, who made graf typos all over the downtown core, come running up to the Jimmy/Assassin with two triple "A" batteries in his hand and says;

-Don't make me restrain you… Pphhzzzzt!-

which the horse throat bettys with broken pagers pointed and chuckled at that.

-I come get my shit tomorrow…you're my fookcin bitch-

says Jimmy and stroles back to the garbage bag fortress under the tree and chats it up with bearded chick with a dick.

-WOh/WOh!!! Am I foockin Citizen!!!!!?-

The chase was to fly the bird to the mystery god. Woht's the lesson of the day? Calculate. What does the math say of the bolts of energy to the ratio of the falling body subdued. The bus stopped and so did Assassin's heart after the jakes came with the 8th 50,000ths'volt to the corpus = …and the coroners report read, "oh well".

2: p1 • 1

{8 cops} 1 Heart stop x the 8th blast?

Do the math… hakim

Naw, H8 got his wisdom. He hears helali spit writs and he pounds his chests in unison… hussaynhussaynhussayn**hussayn**hussayn$_{hussayn}$hussaynhus**sayn**hussaynhussayn hussaynhussaynhussayn**hu**ssaynhus**sayn**hussaynh**ussayn**hussaynhussaynhussaynhus saynhussaynhussaynhussayn**hu**ssaynhus**sayn**hussaynhussaynhussaynhussayn **hussayn**hus**sayn**hussaynhussayn**hus**saynhu**ssayn**hussaynhus**sayn**hussayn**hus** saynhuss**aynhu**ssayn in his livingroom with his bruhs come to sit a spell for their culture; puts rings on his childrens fingers and love them like a commander to his offspring. He controls his collection of stars by working every job imaginable = ol buildings, tearin, building hizs, lifting rocks and slangin math, refurnishing outsides of white trash cycelpathic condos, new construction colonial + unskilled workers, the working poor, line the job, the devoted jazzies = woht's the price of a ticket?¡Ya! comeon homey, tell me.

H8 he's gonna get 1.

…ri…

Evacuation of nuff balling immoral flats empty with blood left on the ceiling. They gone shopping for bathtubs in Hillside — bigga/betta. Runnin. Missions woh/ woh ? wohtever.

Even the one's woht come from a an illdope plan. Bruthaman.

Commission a mission perhaps of cyclepathic collusions and Løcel and H8 wait inna ride peepin the arrival of More approaching. The potholes. Pallo was long gone, naw. H8 attempted to overstand his collusion with Løcel akward cousins akin to rugby and feggotry. Løcel, he still had his scrotes — cook and construction — pushing Indonesians and running game all over the city for cackheads on cane and dealing for coconut popstars who open up to him in phone calls from Norway trying to hook up with his homeboy's roomie. She got dug out at a party when she was 14 on [e] when she her girlfriend split on her and

the dawgs had had a ride. Looky/looky another fookced up Barbie. Party/party. Golly/golly, Løcel still had his scrotes; otherwise H8 would not have given him a 2nd thought.

    Woh Wiggy?

    Woh/woh.

    Fish.

    Woh the diff in this mix is phet view — yute//

    Peacekeepers pictures and Somali kids on digi getting fucked

    while they are stripped dead in angle lust, kid.

Beauty bubble butts with jelly on his back. Photos, posing and prizes. Draggin nagas along for cutting contest ride. A virtual lynch crew. Jumpin dick/phat lips basin the melody of the connection when they kissed. Service providers. Told us and sold us. Each one together on the riding plain. Stake it. Ill dope plans. Woht would uplift each one from schism to the jiz in the feelings. Virtual. Lyrical. Overstanding the collusion of commrads lonely/tourists/bosie/yänkee/workers and ministries/loopypimp gaurds and juvi/rough twinky/cavemen holocaustic mental killer tactricks/

Load up/laptops

Desktop

Digital. Tracks laying. Tying chicas up and training. Gunpowder art work. Pop. Sculpt another whole. Whitebwais and buttons. the mystery of two champs. The emulation of shelf top negowphiles. Pulling on nobs and dials. Come put on and down in the load. A generation fearless and so dying. Roll the cam slowy. Wiggy. The fleshy with modified energy. How could this move them. See the slender of your maybe lover and groove the space twn the breathing with fever — for each other. A busted rubber or raw dealing jammer — more fool the sucka

1: p110 • 3

                              MILK and dIapAs

this is not a mic

    A dolla

    A dup

    A giggle from a duppy

    A dolla to 50.

    50 to dolla

    Fookcen up an element and mixture

    Come holla

Says Løcel,

   -Woht's poppin More-

Says More,

   -Nothin, just chillin-

Says Løcel,

   -Ready to roll, ya-

H8, he kissed his teet and looked straight dead on... for every person... hit the stereo to bump a tune to make the window bounce like a betty getting spanked. Only a vision of of lips in mobility. H8 lived his life straight. His daddy, he only saw H8 on a tilt in his arms maybe twice a week after that and then nada. Beating human breathes into boxes to flexes and sonics, H8 thought the saw his daddy next to him once while pounding his chest, in crowd of bruhs, imaging ezra busting a flow with helali chanting songs of war for his children. B.u.t. he knew it was only a jinn phet he could wrestle for impersonating a memory of energy. Clearity. He stroked his faces and wiped the sweat. The deceptive. Fiddle with the dial yuh sets. Focus the flow through the mess of ecstatic static. He was gone. He was going to listen as Løcel told him of ways to do the rebellion/feed the chillum. Give life to the dawa. A swift calculation. For a father and all the fallen bruthas for all the young fathers. The stars and zoozoos in the kitchen. The addition. All in More; with H8, summed = compliance.

   Says More,

   -coo... ya-listen bro,   *1*

here's the track you asked about
from the top of the long steel stairs.   *2: p67 • 3*
we waited until Walleck fell and fuck
man, that sound drug on for days.
listen, though, the mic's upset still
and swears she pressed play
but she was smoking, and coked   *3: p99 • 1*
and I wanted to say something but
shiiiiiiit she was in that red dress   *4: p163 • 1*
we bought her and it was three stories
up and I didn't want to get what Walleck
got. ashamed? hell no I'm not, what makes
you ask didn't we decide it's art
and so ok? so ok I did try to call once
before the timbre kicked in like fucking
toast popping got no answer. her bags are in   *5: p112 • 1*
the top drawer of the armoire but   *6: p42 • 1*
she's on the dark side now. that   *7: p110 • 2*
I had just checked the corridor clear
myself and maybe not well *toast*.
but I guess there are always more Wallecks
and stairs and haha red dresses. right?
so anyway, bro, throw a backward   *8: p170 • 6*
echo on this shit and the sound will drag
on for days.

later,
rig   *9: p178 • 3*

[Battery Park]

\set1

precious 27 sic; the portholes

moontowel

led

attraction of f(r)ingers

speedoling downlid

some o' the best beebop piana i ever heard

chance is a bag fell outo the bag

the disc

unspun & wandered

blue folk left

1st the ones with little kids

expensive family outing

out being as far out as sitting in a room

with an U.F.O. can

get

just fell outto the mo(u) o ebabs

like toothes with working titles etched invisibly

inta 'em

only abbreviated maybe to untake plaque

for the best charge a minimums   word

help yerself to the fries & wise-ums   *1: p235 • 2*

spotlit(s)

& clean too

insensitive dewguns

sumtime

regraph the caterpultin   *2: p171 • 1*

& in this case only a maestro can claim

the bottom 1/2

ich du 5 iced dinhair muminim &

sleeved short cooled down aftereves

only a pracker knowd the grail

only a SAGA-d shooed the shoit   *3: p122 • 1*

grapple onta livin

garpple inta notes.....

set 2

1: p106 • 2
the vagueries of time

who knew who lived where were

always goes back to 1890s

sheriff street

a tenement w/out shame

this is less than before one could imagine

where is the past now

where is the past now if not

in the head?

2: p57 • 3
or in some book

or map

all museums

all warehouses

whorehouses

windows of rearrangement

this is a story you can tell again &

again

the same way

only different everytime

the grey area of time where "once" is what it's about   *1: p111 • 4*

once i had this white cat

once i had this black dog

erratum continuous tom-tom z-rap

a message of of linels & sinews   *2*

any news

with even a touch of a touched up photograph/still   *3: p54 • 1*

who was/who is

there to the end of christiandom

3 views from the same square

sphere is yes about a continuous line of blowing

rounds

or is it precise corners saught

atemplated shot

as if charted further

here you are slowing down to a star

you'll never catch down to

can we embark in a trump-o-tazzle

or even invectors complete the whole deck

by throwing it over?

the monkey who owned the property's always

the one who flies

1: p103 • 4   & it happens alot between gaps in the mind

& happens it seems around centuries turn.

THE WORLD-FAMOUS TOPEKA ZOO

I ran the answer desk. First job, acne burning.
Only the janitor on work-release had a question:
could he listen to *Aqualung* on my boom box.
The next summer, promoted, I pushed my cart
rattling along the sidewalk, bringing meat
to dwarf crocodiles, *Osteolamus tetraspis*.
The orangutans checked each exhibit latch,
brachiating into their day enclosure,
anticipating the day the gods would slip up.
Hosing down the rainforest walkway,
I looked up in time to glimpse a marmoset
unlatching the door of his cage, and leaping,
splash into the crocodiles' shallow pool.
What seconds of joy, though, mid-air.
Flamingo meant an aunt's hat set on stilts.
Their felt-tip beaks bent heavy with ink,
and their necks spelled *Siegfried Sassoon*.
Beside the keeper's lounge, three white swans
hid, resting beaks in the grass like dress shoes.
By noon it seemed every living thing
wanted to slither, crawl, fly, or brute out.
Vipers were quickest. One day a blind antelope
stumbled through an open gate into traffic.
Some seemed to keep trying after the last try.
The deep freeze help a giraffe's severed face,
staring up from its bag, strangely presidential.
Geckos have civilized the employee kitchen,
crawling up the stucco from behind the radio.
Yet some wallowed and loved. Bottle-raised,
a gibbon reached out long shaggy arms to be held.

1: p177 • 2

2

T———,

Animals are dichotomized into the ones you can shoot
and the ones you can sell. That could be a marmot.
The rivers are all running abnormally high, and the
moribund horse festoons the town with its grim
iconography.

Swatting salmon,
M———

Creature,

This isn't to be marked for errors. After last night, please. I think

1: p195 • 9

Kansas is a fresh deep misery and much more pretty than I once

2

thought. There's the severity, but. I enjoyed our travels. I'm buying
you a book. Remember crossing Mad River? Wyoming? Nothing's

3: p44 • 2

like with you.

Hither,
Yours

4: p61 • 3

Hither,

No score for keeps. First light came; satisfied with reason. If Kansas packs you tight, take off from that aviary: Any mistake hands on a dissimilar connotation. Mad River crossed us, in the insane froth of round trips. I'm ready to read. Send like after like, as harsh as zero.

Creature,
Yours

1

New Orleans, June 3, 2005

Dear S.

Blue glowing squares at 3am. Wet streets sure to turn up French-braided come Sunday   *1*
dawn. And the fish, so energetic!

My one friend/neighbor arrested. MJ sales and possession. Between the last gardening   *2: p81 • 2*
job and this one Christian, God has let there be too much light.   *3: p113 • 1*

Love,
M.

[JFK & Conservatory]

She likes best the orchids with extraneous tendrils — stretched
earlobes, crazy wigs, elaborate tattoos. The hibiscus bred to
resemble the sun low over the ocean. I prefer smell repleting leaves

1: p170 • 8

and balsams fooling across one and other lake latticed light. I wish
I could chunk a buck into the flat gunnels of the brood-blown
punchers. "Half ewe screen the Dalmatians in broom," sheen ax.
"Eye crumb err on sunner end lime ink the grasp. They're the

2: p220 • 2

most beautiful thing in the world."

AEGEAN REDUX

Ivy white as iv(or)y the
Leachianus Giant collects
his echo from the undisputed
king of men, O Susanna won't you

survey a species of shortbread
turning to face the Enso's enzymed
curve—remember you must bow,
she said, before licking
the scalloped rays (off/on)
the lynch pin under David's
juniper berry jam
on toast spears for pastlife accuracy   *1: p112 • 1*

Then it's off to sporks
and plastic saber
key-rattling mop 'n glow
observatory ordinance
logged among carnivorous figs (flies)
figments gone flat

The monastery of Mr. J's
produce aisle English cucumber   *2: p39 • 6*
skin-laden closet
shaves *kanji* from his
thirsty tattoo, the do unto
others demonstrance, the do nothing but
consent (a/e/i = eye) sweep certain
halfway houses that crumble when   *3: p52 • 3*
a drop of *avidia*—protoplasmic
fruit shade adds an Ow, lay off!

That was a warning
from a spotted dune-dwelling spider
don't mind the animation
wombat hangover
slip and slide runway vine
(*digitalis vellum*)
80s pop-up disaster planned
avoidance of emergency exit
red as morning-after powerpoint
make-nice hysterectomy: Zebra, the same
"Z" as in Zyprexa (electrocution happens
HERE

David hid behind
Mona, canary queen
rushed through radiology
1: p195 • 10   with Leachianus (*Leo for short*) under her skirt
2: p170 • 5   hiked high as her fishnets: squiggly bracelet handsewn
etch-a-pad smile (*this time*) with teeth to let them
3: p81 • 2   loose (*giraffes first, sir—Mr. J., you're next*)

LIFERAFT ORDER

4: p55 • 1   and then the girl at Mezzaluna
5: p152 • 1   from the closet—wife—stumbles into delusory
bronchial spasm, sunlight—a common mammalian
lung affect, ischemic condition along with merrily
merrily MERRILY

Vital signs bristling
and League of Topeka Ivies setting up to cross-examine
her ambivalence at the request of Human and Primate Resources
judging by the scene from their internal memo: *water's constitution*
tracking a wrinkled, dilated pupil—*follow the landing gear*
marsupial next of kin
unfolds its penlight across the clipboard's checkboxes

AILIN PENLIGHT

Jack Bommb took the light from his wife's hand. She used to read maps at night. He bellowed like a conductor on a train,

1: p8 · 1

> "FORE!
> BETEL GEUSE!"

and threw it hide and wide.

Did that munchkin penlight pant, "I think I can, I can?" Did it orbit El Tovar, *E. Pluribus Unum* for all to see their source? Did it go round a satellite before the mothership took lumpen home?

> *Where were ye Nymphs when the remorseless deep*
> *Clos'd o'er the head of your lov'd Lycidas?*

That light was like a Wal-Mart beacon whirling to the lost, "come buy, come buy." *Thanksgiving it did not say, "come lay your pence upon mine staring lidless eye."*

2: p176 · 2

The country drunk rewhistled stops. "LOOK OUT BELOW" he cried. It did no good to win honorable mention, except by dispatch to 211. Only Carl Sagan could have so far outspread the sky. But ecoman would later play the slots on Neptune.

Ecoman, Ecoman, only connect. When a Taiwan lady pricks the web a woof erupts on earth. Then rising falls. This call is not an end itself, but one from up above:

> *Stay, stay, stay, stay,*
> *Just a little bit longer.*

Penlight studies show the connected thing. Do their part to shoot the moon. Extend that clip as rudder. Catch the drift. But malfunction forced its prop upon a ledge. It bounced off *a rock like a dodo egg* in the flat nosed dark

3: p172 · 3

> Only connect, connect, connect,
> only connect, connect.

The train ran over the railroad track, but TidBetter did not see the engine crack and he had read *Dark Wind*. Leo opened his mouth. Happy stuffed hers with the primal vox poemato.

Fleas
madam,
Adam
had'em.

Mr. Dag conversed his flask. Lipsy imagined a bath in Nubian arms. Partridge piled dirt between his feet. Another played a tune upon his boot, "I get a kick out of you." The wind chats fidgeted. The zodiac devolved.

More dark came.

Leo finished his wildlife tale. He outwheedled prickly pears.

Spiny or spineless I can't make u up my my y ynd.

Remember that ledge. We're talking dodo egg. Not Einstein. Dodo no read. Dodo look like egg. Be stone. What rock or egg ye know. They did not see the rock invite. Little Lady Taiwan come. Grind powder for her nose.

Slow surface slid to air.

Inertia, that once failed zen, transferred.

Of things that fall one moves.

Le Roi!

The light lay stunned, but the stone egg sailed.

Long live the king,

Down, down dodo fell to Leo's song. Would have smashed him in the head had he not bent over for coffee.

That stone knew more of land than Voyager.

It sang a song of glory.

The stone on mountain's chance of flight! What astronaut saw earth grow big? States of consciousness descried! Not gently into night, it came with fire, sailed Leo's shoulder, hit the saucepan handle.

High upon a mountaintop a stone may dream of flight. This we respect before it hits our heads. But the saucepan neither dreamed nor tried to move.

When the quantum clangs that steady state will change.

And so the saucepan flew.

A black hole flipped quark on Lipsey's front, which stream Newtonicly transferred to mouth.

Tobacco juice shot straight in TidB's eyes.

The saucepan landed on his brow.

The rock then landed in the bed of coals.

Sparks came down. Dark screams roused mules. Picture books gave words.

1

2: p177 • 1

3: p56 • 4

4: p232 • 2

Sparks are falling.
Mules are bawling.
TidB is waving blind.

Grad students fell in all directions. Fire coals took buggies. Phoenix scalped the Patagonian 1: p160 • 3
hump. Who will pay the bill? There is no Jack Bommb in the book.

Shall we send a platitude down? Attach it to a rock? Better the trouble we already caused
before it's worse. How 'bout, "in response to your inquiry that knowledge is now given?" How
about, "Pilgrim Bones?" How about, "Baghdad Come!"

Injections or a pill would serve. 2: p104 • 3

New Orleans, July 28, 2005

Dear S.

1: p41 • 2   Remember when you said you'd bury canned food for me so I wouldn't be afraid of starving?

2   The only neighbor who speaks to me is drunk with teeth. I have somebody's wife or
3   uncle. But he's gone now. Jailed. Friends still selling something worse. An even better
4: p99 • 1   ride if you want to go far.

Love,
M.

DOG HIGHWAY

That highway still fights north
its semis and sedans. Seasons flash.
I age. The dog ran because it was a fool
toward the highway, and I called its name
against the rush, until it stopped,
and sat, on the shoulder's dust,
the way my friend the hunter did not   1
stop climbing hills into state forest shadow
beside a different highway.
What did he find? Sunrise over a peak,
a browsing elk, a sparrow's beak,
an ant's crawl?
I lent a student a book last week,   2: p58 • 1
and she found his *Missoulian* obit,
phlegm-yellow. Letting her
keep the book, I pocketed the news   3: p44 • 2
and it went through the wash,   4: p176 • 4
like most memory. Now
I walk around tame city blocks,
dog on leash, and I say the hunter's name:
Todd. The dog is Lefty. I'm Ed.   5
And your role? You're yourself,   6: p166 • 3
fighting ahead past this moment
highway impatient and blind.

GATHER

1   There was a decision

not to look over

the frozen water
beyond the wall—

2: p93 • 1   the body
already

given over—

nothing reached

Then
one bird pushed open

into migrant snow

3: p110 • 5   and the black throats of hills

took slumber

T———,

There is an entire lot of them. Erstwhile shiny cars,
formerly functional too. Now cinderblocked,
rustpocked. And attended by half a dozen llamas
blinking stupidly. If rustic poverty is scenic, then
yes, it's scenic.

1: p83 • 2

In a state of arrested decay,
M———

T———,

When carbonates precipitate out of solution, they can
form petrified springs. Perhaps mineralized coils.
In the briny lake you'll float high enough to read my
résumé. This is Atlantis in dry dock.

Wishing you'd told me that
before we got off the boat,
M———

T———,

1: p93 • 5

Roadside turquoise is scarce on a Sunday. The fossil beds persist, inaccessible among the brambles and the insects. Intersecting the highway hypotenuse are the wheel ruts of the Oregon Trail. How to dismantle a rattler?

Comparing the swelling to fruit,
M———

2: p102 • 4

Dear Grady,

1: p59 • 1 I am your red dress girl, shit-man, get outta here and all, knee flounce kicked up in the rain and everythin else. My last fill, the last stop on this highway, all prettied up in Jean Nate after wipin *2: p195 • 7* down greasy windowsills, the day's dirt scraped out from under my nails, touched up and pink, but mostly don't matter. *3* I do the way you think, all rowdy and bendable. I hold a lot. It's the ugly ones I like though since they don't remind me of you none. They come on *4: p75 • 1* all strong and talk like and then nothing but little boy in their eyes once we're alone, and the whole time thinkin in those dingy rooms with the blinds drawn and the hum of the ceiling fan that I watch sometimes till it blacks me out with spin, that there is sun on top of all this and I sure hope my dead mama ain't watchin me right now. She'd thrown her hands up and wrung her hair with too much care bout me. I held those hands in the end and tell her it weren't her fault. She was still speakin then, but didn't say nothin just fixed me in her eye and then they seamed shut imagin the next life I suppose, and she started moanin and rockin. I guess I upset her again, as I always did and this way how least she'd come to be free of me. And you're free of me except like a whisper hairlash in your eye you keep pullin at, I'm still there, figurin I guess you'll come back *5: p58 • 1* down this road. I'm rememberin you lookin *6* at me nice that time at Slappy's and my dress *7* before it tore. Remember *8: p163 • 1* Grady doncha? I'm here. It's okay. It's mended now. Yours, still and all,

Lo-Red

Dear Lo,

Do you still sniff chemicals at work when you clean the restrooms? Better   1: p61 • 3
on top of the box than out there behind the big asthma door. You know
they put a green powder in the tissue paper of this hotel. They put three   2: p90 • 3
tablespoons in and I swallowed three. It was bad. I almost died and with…
Grady? He said I smoked his last joint and afterwards kept asking why the   3: p59 • 5
shower wouldn't…. It was too old a hotel. Maybe you cleaned it before he
cleaned…? There was that star that he taped to my shirt. That star was a
church. It echoes right here. The funny thing was that it didn't even take
cops to break us up. Someone came to the hotel room. One cop knew
about the echo. He was tripping his partner out and then Grady left. You
know how it is—if you bend down and put your ear in the groove of a
man's belt you can hear the echo? I didn't even know until the cop showed
me. It was like that with Amii—no not *that* Aimii. *That* girl is crazy too.
She's always wearing grizzly bears on the top of her head. She's got quite
a few kids. But with *this* Aimi—she goes out with Z—it's like multiple kids   4
at the same time. She was on the lawn the other day looking for juice. She
found it but she didn't know where to get her kids back to after she dank.
They could have come to church, I told her. The services would have ended   5: p141 • 1
well before kickoff time. But she kept asking about you.

Did Matt use up the whole Sunday?

Louve,

Dar   6: p39 • 3

WHEN THE LAW COMES

1: p195 • 1

2

3: p35 • 2

4: p170 • 1

5: p143 • 4

When the law comes I will tell them we are apples. They'll laugh at this and then bite. The law will wear redblue sweaters with doves stapled onto them giving a wingflap or a squawk at appropriate moments but otherwise feigning death. Darla, when the law comes you will hide in the sink faucet and I will not offer them water no matter how often or how conspicuously they allude to their thirst buds. I will tell them they should have drunk natural truck juices with high fructose computers before they dared put boots on the ground as they say. When the law comes I will spit in their faces and tell a dirty apple joke. They will pretend to understand but in fact they won't. When the law comes with their bodies full of worry and fresh wild morals and when they tie their long blond hair back in short tight dollars and when they announce they are here to make us more competitive you like I said will hide in the sink faucet and I will try to entertain them and they will playact for thirty or so versatile seconds and then they will shoot. Yes it will hurt because it has to hurt. Bartender, I will say to the doctor, stop here on red, no turn on red, and he will laugh knowingly, and he will not stanch the bleeding. When the law comes you will urge me by the elbow and say some beans don't fart but I will stay put. Darla, I will say, we'll always have Monaco. That will put some tears on your cheeks hence the faucet. When the law comes and yes the law will come, I will say to them the snake was just here before you. You know they feign fearlessness but watch how they'll get careful with every redblue footstep and pray for their troops. The snake was just here, I will repeat, the snake was just here before you, I will say when the law comes.

Fairhazel Gardens, 1: p85 • 2

I am under the chair. See half a monarch wing in the dustbin.
Backyard vixen squalled all night to her cubs. No need to look 2
outside, but I did. Red apple with a broken neck. *Every word is an* 3: p40 • 1
unnecessary stain. Take back your eyes. Remove an ant from your 4: p165 • 1
arm without snuff. I am under the phone book which is under the
wheel. I'm in an earth, call-less.

Swift,
Dutch Flat

1: p99 • 4   Dear Z,

2: p62 • 3   One always fails to find a shutter that's been making the noise everyone hears and no one can find.

3: p80 • 1   What—happens—here—between—these—beginnings.

Feng shui advocates avoiding L-shaped homes because there are many areas missing.

4: p1 • 2   Did she say *sperm coffin*?

It may be earlier, after noon.

New Orleans, September 8, 2005

Dear S.

Haven't managed to get a package off to my heroin addict. Then again he too must   *1: p112 · 3*
experience the strange sense of time.   *2: p106 · 1*

Sleeping upside down on an armchair for months. The geography I am learning.   *3*
Should I drive out and get you? I think I may be leaving things out.   *4*

Love,
M.

EXCESS CONCEPTIONS MEDITATIONS RAPIST

fighting venomous bile
as dawn uncoils
1   the bodies breathing still

the black tooth poisons sleep with a flicker

2   Technicolor feed in the colloid static

NOTICE

3   *The indications and dosages of all drugs have been recommended in*
the medical literature   conform to the practices of
community.
specific approval   use in
     diseases and dosages
                 it is advisable to keep abreast of revised
recommendations   new drugs.

discontinuation

complex-partial

duration

of 400 mg/day

the same mysterious sentences appear

A reliable history must always supplement the mental

target symptoms

twenty-four years and some odd

daze

i lie awake

i nake with unicorns

on white horse everything

the shape bears crude teeth

gulps mad apples out of nowhere

arguable

abrupt attempts whatever

a way to deal with boredom

i am so   i am so slowly

into the greygreen sea that swallows

1: p191 • 1

2: p177 • 8

3: p103 • 1

4: p195 • 1

5

the latency of response

status examination

1: p152 • 6

bizarre behaviors usually

is greater than 5 days

occurring more

work

5. Baseline of premorbid functioning

2   *and float*   6. *Time. . .illness*

7. History of prior response

8. Family History

bury yourself

3: p59 • 3   be aware of side effects

emulsion

dry mouth and blurred vision

4: p3 • 2   an open wound

someone on the other end

obsessing

i am a pine cone

i don't want October to end

5: p79 • 2   the message

avoid additive toxicity

secret personal appeal

syndicating layer

from the American   a muse

document observations

distinguish these colors

screaming

X-es

i don't know what it is
it has pages but is not a brochure

1: p25 • 4   perplexity at the height of syndrome

history or affective disorders
2   *a population that abuses laxatives and diuretics*

difficulty with concentratio   *time of day*
impulsity   *obsessions and*   *compulsions yes*
target responsive

3   the demonish attraction
coax the moon out from her
4: p193 • 5   pyromania

the largest category
        peculiar to himself

       absorbed on the downpour
singing   always
            the deep-toothed leaves
       the variable thickets

1: p67 • 8 # THE RIVER IS FAR BEHIND US

'her eyes . . .

2   she's on the dark side . . .'

3: p75 • 8   a dub echo effect i.e. ' (((((('
4: p104 • 1   massive corridor maze of PCP

the dead fish in his head / gentle

treetop variations

a window on birdsex

hangs by one clawed foot

her metal cage or mango tree sunlight

5   (wellers hill soaking a blue bag in the dark

collected wooden objects

6: p67 • 1   part of his leg under the cyclone wire concrete

7   rain eating toast

at the window /

8   inertia

comes in silence

9: p112 • 7   suns a dirty secret

something out of town   is so

he lingers)

talking to a skull

THEY

When some from a corner   I saw it in a doorway, I   *1: p12 • 1*
thought I saw a door

Because I know her house   and thus think of it as age

Only recently have ghosts been people we never knew   *2: p67 • 6*

Because once I lived here too   *3: p16 • 2*

Once I lived   *4*
entirely at night
and because it was during a heat wave, the power went out. We lived an
entire week in the dark
heat.   *5: p27 • 3*

A bright
bridge in the fall. The back of the wrist
breaks its wing

in its little then
it makes a sun

which adds up to them.

THE MAN WHO ATE BREAKFAST FOR DINNER

He had recently become interested in the habits of Albert Einstein. He particularly relished the knowledge that the scruffy old genius disliked wearing socks. He himself disliked wearing socks and walked around his new house barefoot, trailing dirt in from the yard. Feeling the ground with naked feet was important to him—it was a reminder of the apparent solidity and certainty of the sphere beneath. He appreciated the cold hardness of the earth in the evening, even as he knew there was nothing solid, his only certainty now being the infinite mystery of the universe as it vibrated in separation and unity.

He enjoyed his solitude at night. The gradual comfort he would feel in the sense that nothing existed in him. Wet toast on the windowsill. And the darkness beyond. The absolute absence of singularity.

In the morning, often before the sun was up, he could be found in the yard standing perfectly still, reflecting on the change in his circumstance; his newfound ability to breathe. That was the time for looking up. He did not believe in god or heaven but had faith in the universe. The sky was part of a promise he had made to this new incarnation. He would face its expanse every morning and ride the suggestion of its limitlessness into its evaporation. The daily ordeal was a comfort of sorts. He no longer used, but it was hiding in the shadow of every moment. Sometimes he could hear the blistering of his skin as he allowed a tongue of prior desire to trace a thin line down the back of his neck. He could close his eyes and remember. Shoulder blades pushed together, body contorting, he could taste the building hunger, feel the creature stir. He forced his eyes open. He watched the darkness leach, bleed green into the leaves. To see this itself ushered some sense of warmth under his skin. First things first. There was coffee to brew. After that, there would be something else. This was the method now. Day by day. Moment by moment. Eventually, there would be socks to put on. As long as he remained barefoot, there was always something more to do, a sense of purpose. With the coffee brewed and the strong aroma bolstering him, he might sit in the battered old chair in the yard for hours, not reading, not writing, just thinking, preparing for something that would have to be done. Preparation was important. It was necessary for him to negotiate himself through the day. Up north, the day advanced slowly, in no particular rush. Mornings loitered namelessly, like vagrants in hand-me-down shades of midday. There was no blinding heat, no excuse for a noon retreat to sleep, no cover for a dirty secret, a treacherous lover. He thought about his old yard, in a place far south, a place that had to be left behind. His old yard had two avocado trees joined by a hammock. Behind the hammock, his beehive hummed, brimming over with simmering sweetness. A bird of paradise bobbed lazily at one end of the hammock.

He had miniature orange trees. Lemon trees. Splashes of bougainvillea spilled over the fence and the sun blazed mercilessly into the morning with bright contempt for whatever tragedies the night had entertained. It was a blinding existence. Excruciating to see such beauty and know it was all out of place. He could do nothing but inhale his escape: melt it, roll it carefully between his fingers, shut out the light and draw in. Now, there was no more escape. That had all been left behind. It wasn't explained. It would not be explained. It was one day without and then another, a journey outward and a matter of not returning, no more singularities to hide away in. *Schwarzschild.* He felt a quiet satisfaction at knowing the name of black holes before they were black holes. He knew that to some black holes were a transcendent beauty, a merging of time and space and a loss of individuality. But they were also compositions of collapse and destruction. Einstein had lived in a universe without black holes; he had a strong emotional aversion to the idea and simply decided that he didn't want them in his world. It was Einstein that made the world of black holes a possibility and yet he held firm in his refutation. Sitting in a chair in a yard all day was part of a similar determination. He sat in his new yard all day long, preparing for the day. Sometimes it took a great deal of preparation. As the darkness began to dull the luster on the leaves, calming the chatter, soothing the sense that things must be done, he was ready to make it through the day. He rose from the chair and walked to the kitchen. He filled a bowl with cheerios and ice cold milk, set the toaster, and stood alone in the center of the room, some wordless jazz meandering from the radio he never switches off. Finally, he succumbed to the urge and allowed one foot to tap along with the sound of another man's meditations.

1: p150 • 3

2

3: p178 • 8

4: p110 • 8

[Norfolk & Delancey]

(for (e) shadow)

tell this   dy /// nam   is   mos

useless blues & pinks

in mentus

this is daylight when we most need it when

there is no day left

this is river in a shadow

shadow against an even/ing when

tree become sky

no mental can the shadows stay this silent for so>long

1: p186 • 1   the bricks that never saw the war they fought for

it is a yellow in the eye

useless magenta that crosses our lives

the sun is behind me the sun

            it heats my neck

dy na mis mos   contrarios

           one

immigrant says to another

      i passed thru here

(too)

       vialavitsef   feast   & live

       tale tail's tale   to   taste

        aventus   creatus

rowldtercompat

the act of natural act of..................

       i've come

thru here too

       the shadows

never move

                     the trees &

sky are one

                    glass & stone

& steel a blding make

                    fingers make

things happen

one immigrant says to another

                glass stone &

steel

                  are the

building blocks of this world

trader trapped inside the gullum

is a wink   the paper asleep

i crumble

        in uniform your day begins

   like this: shadows never move

        sun behind your back

        useless magenta

bricks that tell a tale

fingers make things happen

running spotlights cannot function before the nite arrives

it is really not the clock that determines transition

that crosses our lives

          one immigrant says to another

      it is when the sun crosses our backs like a river

   a festival   a

world -

        sonic   tellin   panic

      when the light that was created

     becomes the light that was invented

   a bet earned   a wise trade   a gorge traversed

2(money   is the (M) angle

   we will not be fed by sunlight   a   loan

     even now as evening turns   snurt the concessions

no time for this/that   it's obligat(o)ion

0bliGate

it's now dark it feels

one immigrant says to another

feel my neck   it passed this way

this is no joke

privitize my sacrament it's cool now hands on it's cool now

1: p57 • 4   the useless magenta adds to the piano's song

this world was built by hands

tree & sky no longer touch

the shadows have become a river

that does not flow

brick is what i call your face

i remain attached to my allegiance

tea is a drink for two (3)

this shifting desire is a wedge

between the   clock & the hrs

clamusin   tourista   raditsula   bo   ard

such useless appendages these hands against the unmanacled day.   *1: p162 • 8*

TURNTABLE INTERROGATION TECHNIQUES

The dubbwoys rush the playground.

Viddy this, they hear and run forward. When do you belong in Us? Hear this. Feel. This dub is Us. They come to rumble like that. The PhatbaKs and heretics never hestitate to put a duppy on it's back.

Pop

Drop

Ardbop = fade, segue, break, mix, fookcup the duppy and scratch, sample and bang on the ivories like those Chi-town selectors.

We're in the Hiz, gawd.

Send the message out to fail the confusion.

-...done slip, Bruh...

move, Bruh

shatter the windows of whips, Bruh-

In the beginning was the word and the word was bass. And the bass was good and Gawd saw that it was good and Gawd said and Gawd left plenty. Gawd left notes and files and jams and cycles... and Vico saw that Homer saw and Virgil heard and cyphered the story of blindness and loss of self and he turn Us all into brave warriors who feared nadathin, and refused to forget and stepped to fate like like yänkee and fadayee,

-Comeon, I nah fear ¡Ya! never, you and y'crew-

Play the jam cross Somalia-Blocks. They fixed the speakers up in doorways and windows.

Black to Blackey and forthe to Gawd's messengers

Ardbop,

Oi, yo, Tre!

Please

Please

Please

See the riddim race in accustic space.

Jam the duppy down. King fix your dome on your Brutha's selection. Steady yourself. Balance = table.

Flag the needle.

Done slip

Blocks are your lab.

Phatbaks mash the mad/mean from the music.

LORD

Gosh!

     Golly!

and pray Gawd,

          G is.

Give this music to the def and breath this naga shit in, Bruh.

...zooga zooga zooga zooga zooga zooga zooga zooga zooga zooga zooga zooga

...zooga zooga zooga zooga zooga zooga zooga zooga zooga zooga zooga zooga

...zooga zooga

...zooga zooga

...zooga zoog

...a cotton candy jelly woobly boobly hackie sack stretches and bounces over the playground. It jets out silver shimmery discs which land on the ground spinning. The children rush them crack

Crackity   crack

       Crack   crack

   Crack   pop

               Each kid what steps on one is bit mapped into bits of fleshy

They hurried more quickly and the cracking of discs and blasting of flesh went up a levels more...

Crackity   crack

       Crack   crack

   Crack   pop   and the bats come and fly and blast apart as they get attracted the sounds of kids in collision.

          Pop

   phzzzzt

      phzzzzt

  phzzzzt   *.....BOOOOMM crack*

Pop   pop   pop

   Pop

        pop

     ...bursted up in the air they wreck and **ka'put** like human rockets — demolished — disassembled homies blasting into gooey popcorn each cry has no treble...

     Crack   crack

   Crack   pop

        Pop

Crackity   crack *phzzzzt*
          phzzzzt
phzzzzt
          Crack   crack
Crack
          bust blasted kids and bats
Pop   pop   pop   Crackity   crack
          Crack   crack
Crack
                              Pop

                                   pop

...till they gust all the discs and make the grounds into a carpet of diced meaty fruit
jelly -assembling the zone to the nontoxic mit out soundbwais
                    ...let loose the sonic.
                    So then the phaylanx step forward fingering the generalz and
devilz and the dubbwoys rush
the duppy empirical...
          nonvisual
                    bass and clearity
                    woofers...

...zooga zooga

...zooga zooga

...zooga zooga

1   *sssshhhhhhoooo'q*

One time for your mind, puta.

          Que pasa! ¡Que, Rifa!

          Whatelse can an Island bwoy do to destroy America?

          Mightys from E-Town to the Hood come to rumble the duppy at George Jay. Maybe
all the lils could dream within their self as a carpet of bouncy muck; regulate and save the
daye.

          Did Jimmy say that all songs start with a cry?

                    ...when i look at you, i see the enthusiastic appearance of the great army...

Pullin trains on the 14th degree

                    ...when i look at you,

These Gawdz of thunder

                    ...when i look at you,

Lords of of the wasteland

                    ...when i look at you,

These are the hollow bwoys

...when i look at you,

The tuff bwoys

...you will see it with your eyes...

With the gesture of this dusty hand

I command you to get your bands to stand

Hi Tec Wab — The Ghetto bassy, G

This is the Fuchx

¡Ya!

Hi Tec Wiggaz

This is the Tek

¡Ya!

Hi Tec Hooliganz

This is the Army

¡Ya!

Hi Tec Ninja

This is Cream

¡Ya!

Hi Tec Super Sane Nekgah

This is the GottiJinn

¡Ya!

Hi Tec Go Black

This is the Lil Burg

¡Ya!

Hi Tec X-ray Yush

This is the No

¡Ya!

Hi Tec badup slow flow Poro

This More

¡Ya!

Hi Tec Ras Gawd

This is woht was one more

Their tashbir morph into chains and attach themselves to breast jinns
pulling ready for attack.

4.

Done miss a beat

Done miss a beat

Chaotic theories of urban wreck em up = each one a go to coshin each one.

Bring Us up to this heretic jam

Mainland disconnected

Clash the wicked

> *...for every person there is a driver and a witness*

Tre

Illhuman beat box it

Ardbop, juggle the mixer

Lay a plate with a track from the planet of the Irps

The Nekgaz fuse to the 1 = 1 aim +1 destiny.

> *...snakes take baby steps...*

the nation takes a giant

Knowledge + Wisdom = ?

Think for Me.

> *...my themes are tactical snapshots...*

The transformation of samples is your room become yuh yard — reassembling to make a proper plate — this block becomes a party in resistance amplified to echo Woht weapons? We use to bomb wallz with skillz now we roll bombs like a kill

> *And if in all respects unequal, be capable of eludin them.*
> *A lil crowd is but a mark's grip for one more Mighty.*

...anticipate the reaction or the resistance of the enemy...

Our equipment

> Flanger, fists and pirate digital.

> > *choppin up ...my themes are tactical*

> *the snapshots...*

> *...anticipate*

...the resistance of the enemy...

> > > > s'ound clash

The beat drops as sneaky as a stealth bomber. Ardbop flips his fingaz over the plates and feels the scarred wax on his tips gliding over the grip from the residue of helium and then he twist his wrists

> Steady

Go steady like a bassy. It jazzy. King Tim! stay ready. ...play back the transcript of Gotti... Tre, he's the telepathic sound system selector, dun. Dappah Ardbop's digits shreddin this riddim in waxy pores. He mad hecktic the sequencer/yän

> > > > kee.

He made a plate for this — to move the Heretics to crash y'crew.

> Is this on the real?

Massive black kids with dawgbwai s on car chains circling the square.

> Baboons bitch slappin pittbulls for the muslims who greys once called coons.

Equalize youself Mightys and regulate

Fail the fate of massive confusion

Ovastand this dubwise collusion of bands of homebwoys soon to see the bassy.

G'¡Ya! say

Slam the sonic.

Oh what a mess... Dans become hysterical with the grapple in the metaphysical =
the duppy is a soundbwoy!

   Transformation to the physical *will make you feel the pain the we experience*

Woht did louis say?

     Big boom

     From under the ocean

1000s gone = millions on the MOVE

       Raw/tambran

    wham/bam/

    [b]//waaah/

boom// boom/boom/boom

Boom/boom

   Boom/boom

...the pain the we experience...

  Move it over, dawg, dang

       yaeh

Aow

   pleeeeease

     I guesss I was helping her...

Ardbop and Tre cue quick to clock the dawg, build or employ the techniques
of the Grand Master. Flash is... Flash got a blaster on his head like Poros to the
Grand Master.

Extreme failures = rude dudes with ratchets at their speakers.

    Tek comes rushin up with a giggle dog as his slave and ripps off his
muzzle turning the rudies into levas then he sets the beast jinns to devours the
soundbwais and their thugz yet they cannot die. *...try another vein... I guesss I was
helping her...* Men with Metal detectors walked about in a trance spottin rigs and
coins in the yards of recreation and the 3 topless Janes kept levelin Cain.

  the stripping of

*breasts — and milk rushes out and drowns out the sound of screaming faithfuls and likkles
til Lil Burg gets his jinn to chomp a chunk of meat from the jug and slash the kneck of the
daemons with a tashbir transformed from chains. He holds a word in script by No. It's a
page from a 5 Star Blue Note Book:*

**'Walls filled with grafs like calo
typos/the sacred texts undissed by
the purified locos'**

these are words from...

turntable interrogation techniques

6.522...these are the effects which cannot be made into flows:

The duppy went to swallowing seeds again and wombles
danced and wombles danced waving hammers at jets as the bananasplits roll by
lookin snorky inna dip ride bangin spedding murdered by tubby then Fuchx saw
a version. It was plate of More out by Goldstream drenched in lighter fluid and
smoke ash. There were sparks of living light plucking the hairs from his body.
More special, he, stepped into a frame — stood on a cliff of blood burned into
clay which became tile. The running streams became a hallway and the kids busted
there noses and ripped their lips slamming themselves into walls. Wiggy was dancing on the lunch table as the warders and cyclepaths clapped and laughed. Some
kid had a rocket launcher aimed a speaker on the school wall. Under a table a na-
tive kid with headphones typed sparks like letters from a latop making the illusion
of logic dutch Schultz math tricks into paratatic sentences transformed into news
items made music.

Wittengen saw Abbas as the genius of gringo coshin commando communiqué
centrifugal numerics strategy.

Literacy performance art was made on the real by bum rushin the 999th plateaux
givin way to philisteens

Squared in 4 elements of dark skinned arabics

Or island kids armed with throw lighters and pipe rockets

Fuchx with a heart like a forked sword splits opponants headshells

Striking barers and banners of fear

The courage of an armless soldier

Bringing warrior's water

Truht and not delusion.

...lackin in schoolin...

yet producing the sonic discussion of the x-ray vision

the stripping of

treble

these are words from...

Fuchx saw a More special in the science room using gun powder and oil to
smooth over the wounds and eczema — covering his knot. The dub was
scratchin. He saw More being downloaded by SMUs, jakes, sailors and ministry
workers as a cowboy previewed mpegs of Wiggy stripping the Mighty...

bass

turntable interrogation techniques

exploiting phobias,

He saw More's mom crawlin on the floor car chained to a dawgbwai pullin her
legs as she collected and reassembled pieces of shatterd geisha masks.

    ...taking away comfort items

    Fuchx with a heart like a forked sword splits opponants headshells

Striking barers and banners of fear

          down

with the courage of an armless soldier

Bringing warrior's water

    leadership & firmness

    heroism in the hiz

    700 hearts filled with faith

Woht's the weight of the world?

    ...bass...

    ...taking away comfort items

    The texte of the 5 Star gon a x-ray

a shadowed figure swang from a plum tree

1.2.

1   2

victoria see nagas and all eyez get lynchy

...trebling pon sensitivities.

    ...gimme my try...

          cracked masks with salt stains

hymens busted in trains

    Dred Don Dane covered the Blue beat dream — postered the scene all over the city.

    Punctuated by the visual liquid compositions of I.B.C.

    Sound systems as resistence fighters with light weapons

Army see his daddy. Army see his moms. Army see her face filled sampled with
kaposi

    ...ring around the rosy....

    Coke mules and career opertunities for children like homosexuals and the
teenage prostitution.

    ...what's his math? He's such a cutey...

    From the Bowery to Hells Kitchen or sussin the grow stashed on
reservations.

    Come MighTY lord duke Fuchx and say,

        STEP UP!!!

Come flex...

Smackin crack sots in the Holiday with Billy.

S'all jus nega shit, gree.

[Hit it with the illhuman heretic King Tim drum machine]

Tre.

Ardbop reloads

And he reloads

And he reloads

Chasin pitch to balance the revolution of fads — held in ransom with twice the power to sacrefice, these Mightys, holdin down their square, are as solid as 10 thousand with the force of a fid

...ready 2...

1.2.

1.2. transforming the block into a hiz come to party. Bruthas. Esquires. Purify with fire.

Gang bangin the duppy with the will of fadayee

hear,

here:

the reach the reach the reach the reach the reach the reach the reach the reach...

Cream is stalled and surrounded by giggles, deadeyes and smirks as he gets boxed in by walls of webpages. His throw lighter tumbles. He sees only massive digits of megs and plungers, endless downloads and More being sucked up into upload files and completed folders. Holocustic holographic local ganked pornographics being devoured by baboons and beast jinns chompin on geisha masks. He sees the transcripts of endless chats with homosexual sociopaths and dialogues of entramp-ment. He sees a grey fat man in James bay watching a naga bwai get fucked on a couch by pox festered pale man who is nude under a cowboy hat and construction workers shooting dope up their arms in the livingrooms of federal workers.

Gawd.

The birth of confusion.

Fusion.

Bombin the walls of building. Old and new school. This Island. More. Aaron.

...and dub babys raised by romans. Breakin hymens and definitions. An ill dope plan...daddies dreaming jism mixed down to sets transformed from semen = rhineland bastard

in creation

The deadeye men. Jinns. Ins.

The illin beginning...

Ah radiant chillum

technology invasion nad the ragamuffin cousins with a hidden pocket full of local product — massive technology = Meth crystals poppin geishas maskies

jus try and clock Me

...sssshhhhhhooooch zuuq

Stroll passing in a broken beat cop...

...zooga zooga......sssshhhhhhooooch

Lil burg dream/dream/water it drip like everywhere ...like the trickle down the side of mental — posses and possibilities ...iced in the middle of two crackers pretending to be pissed over a betty.

Clip a brutha stuck in the center.

...ring around the rosey...

Lil burg sees the back of a image of a boy's head kinky on his knees...

hands cuffed and a weapon at the back of his natty. It looks kinda picturesque like a movie or groovey like top shelf cd homicide darky bwais. Mag pockets standing, without motion, behind him, at stations somewhere. the face of the baldy obscured by flesh distortion of metal disruption as the body sinks deep in the ocean....

...gotti...

The deadeye men. Jinns. Ins.

The illin beginning...

Ah radiant chillum

We crash y'crew/Gats on Dats/Woht weapons? /Our weapons/Tardid or Repitition. Swords and words spoken/Our identity/7:30 irony: the balance of the needle, arm and turntables

...and sturm and drag queen troopers bust butts over the heads of kids trying to build castles out of pebbles and make them play jump rope with tied used condoms as bombs blast the playground to shreds.

ah

...sssshhhhhhooooch zuuq

Stroll passing in a broken beat cop...

...zooga zooga......sssshhhhhhooooch   ,

Was's moms was down to a few pounds, by then, and hanging out at the
Max on the corner early morning before the sun come red fa down
and when others set to prey and some pray....
Their flow will bring urban tales like cantos
Of the glory of grafs on walls
Of locos with spray can type
Oh oh oh that
New Palestinian tag...

...and some feggit, when Army was 12, he tried to fuck with Army and

the yänkee shankt the subject 1 night and dumped him inna bush — the

likkle Mighty kept walkin like, s'all la = mind/no matter.

...but he loved his uncle harlo

come sing me a tale of the ol school

crews

like Tek's daddy and the Danny Boys

Spoony Gee vs Giovanni's radical scribbles

Silence the duppy's giggles

Swang Poro,

Just like Woht Was

No,

Fuchxmo,

Lil Burg

GottiJinn

Creamfist inna paralysis

Army and Tek

They come to wreck

...zooga zooga......sssshhhhhhoooooch

the stripping of

the body

exploiting phobias

the body

these are words from...

the riddim

ya aba abdillah

nahnu ummat in the hiz...

turntable interrogation techniques

Typing luv/love letters to martyres and timothy macvie

...taking away comfort items

walyi

...a system of turntable interrogation techniques, habibi

to treble pon sensitivities.

[mmammm]

nice

[MmMmmm]

Gawd is.

                                        knowin
        clay struggle with fire
        protected from the poets
                Surrounded by water. Let Ardbop build the pyre. He got a
riddim to drop so throw it — on the masses. drop the the wicked on their
faces. ...*bun yah...* He twistin some tempos and fuckin with the flanger
and echos...
                kinda slapback
whispers
                        angered angels
yells
surround the waddy's proximity
                        we duckin
                        Jakes
now ain't that wicked
mics and bikes

never break
                for snakes
ah for heavensake
                Stompin feet and feelin kai

        kiss me kneck!!
                watch them step
heavy heavy
                into the stanza
strong
                        Brutha Ardbop pulled the Trane and said,
                "*Maybe Our voices is suppose to crack as you meet your*
                maker in song."
the stripping of
                exploiting phobias
        these are words from...
        Ardbop's turntable interrogation techniques
        Wreckin up phobias,
                ...a sound system of turntable interrogation techniques
                that was in part woht was unbassed
                finger grooves and wax...

and trebling pon sensitivities —
heavy heavy
enemy of the republic
                    spits
ebonics and sonic
            cypher
all yuh bet = black boys punk you like thamud/with wiggas and chugs/holding
back mad boy dawgies/skinny jinns/strapt to car chains transformed to tashbir.
The transformation... These are the Dubwoy/ mashin up sets of duppies at the
George Jay—

1   *Play>*

¡YA!   *YA!*   *YA!*
              Ya!
                       YA!   *YA!*
YA!
                    -...ri-
         -G¡Ya!-

WOOP!   **WOOP!**
      Woop!
           -Steady, yänkees. Stronge We strong, ¡Ya!-
WOOP   WOOP!   WOOP!
           WOOP!   WOOP!
                              WOOP!
      -six up-
           -peace out-

1: p176 • 3

[Carlo & Calle Real]

gold's gym, santa barbara, 1989

breaking news across the treadmills states cooperating with kuwait authorized to use *all necessary means* the wall is down reunification set *vogue* your step-aerobic thong madonnas bethesda gene therapy bay bridge collapse goodbye margaret thatcher hello implant contraceptive nc-17 spotted owl tree sitters sandinistas out civilization lemmings prince of persia metal gear supermario zelda final fantasy streetfighter first female president of central america in other news placido domingo pavarotti *past their prime* mapplethorpe obscenity kevorkian betrays hippocratic oath hubble telescope launched mandela freed *they won't be singing that song anymore* killer bees johnny carson leaves tonight marion barry blows passing through the tunnel under the highway grafitti *rush FIJI* kilroy wuz here *the cure* black clothes pointy shoes *be all that you can be* white stars blue field undulating stripes *bush is pro-choice* over which a wire hanger superimposed

[Ocean & Ashton]

ocean avenue 24-hour fitness, san francisco, 2005

breaking msnbcfoxcnnnews across the treadmills coalition of the
willing not *my* president suicide bomb beheading you're evil axis *hung*   *1: p184 • 1*
up or *hang up and drive* your ipod bluetooth unconstitutional same-sex
bay bridge fiasco supersize me cialis madonna blast kills wedding party
lord of war lord of the rings harry potter star wars chronicles of narnia
woman elected leader of germany in other news extreme infotainment
makeover situation room hummer h2 clinical trial results in permanent
injectable wrinkle filler schwarzenegger terminates tookie grand theft
auto halflife halo burnout 3 total war fable *dear sir i solicit your urgent*
help from nigeria what would jesus do intelligent design google weapons
of mass destruction *error: page not found* astrodome a scene of horror
goodbye johnny carson richard pryor o'reilly invites terrorists to blow
up coit tower graffiti art at moma african american *army of one* white
stars blue field *red glare* hoist flag at ground zero

1

GIVE PETE A CHANCE

2

The war is about to begin and I'm looking at a flyer, a list of all the countries America has ever gone to war with, a long list. I can't hear my phone because of the crowd, so it isn't until she's ten minutes late that I go outside to check my messages. One message.

'Hey, I'll be late.'

She'll be late. I go back into the bar because it's raining and end up in the stairwell. People pass me and give me the eye. I give them the sorry look. It's getting late and she's still late so I call her.

'Hello?' she answers.

'Hey it's Pete, where are you?'

'Eating.'

'Where? I'll come find you.'

'6th and Mission.'

We're on the same corner. I pan around, all Thai and Vietnamese. I ask her which restaurant. The sound of chewing, Thai. 'Stay there,' she says. 'I'll be over in five minutes.'

'Just tell me which restaurant.'

'It's best if you wait.'

There's the stairwell and then where the bathroom vents its smells. Fuck, it's crowded. The more I wait, the angrier I get. Pushed around to the edges by all that movement, waiting for some girl with a food problem. I leave.

The train is fast and loud. I plug my ears with my fingers. My back is tired from wandering the city all day. I'm sick of the city, my dumb job, my small room. I want to leave, but you can't leave when nobody's asking you to come. I don't want to turn into one of those old city guys who lives in a room, smells funny, and has only his superior knowledge of jazz to feel good about.

3: p38 • 3 Thelonious Monk my ass. Find me a woman, move to a small town, ride a bike, learn to cook, read in the afternoon.

The escalator lifts me into the rain, lit against a black sky. Cities do not have stars. They're all on the streets—or at least they think they are.

I enter the perpetual mist and call Al.

'What's up?'

'Where are you? I'll come find you.'

'Elbo Room.'

'I'm coming over.'

'Yeah.'

Al's at the back of the bar, a black mound under dim red lights. The table, covered with empty glasses. The answer: rum and Coke. Always.

1: p143 • 1

I tell Al the thing with the Thai food, the chewing thing. He spits out a cherry stem. Then this old woman, a sad drunk, sits down at our table. She's missing a tooth and wearing flannel. A smoker, I can tell by her skin. Al answers her questions generously. She touches my arm and I ignore her. Embarrassed and hurt, she leaves.

2: p56 • 1

'What's your deal?' Al says.

'Nothing.'

'Everybody says nothing but everybody needs something.'

Everybody needs a clever friend. That's what I wanted to say to him.

3: p212 • 1

The last N-Judah is always the best, empty of people and full of newspapers. The headline says we are going to war. I'm lying down across the seats, a chest warm full of liquor. I close my eyes and she's there. Too many girls, not enough brain cells, not enough change. She'll call tomorrow and explain herself, or I'll explain myself. Doesn't matter who's explaining, as long as somebody's wrong.

IF WHAT CAN CHANGE THEN EVERYTHING CAN CHANGE

§§§§

Is that it?

Like on Seinfeld when the dentist is Jewish for the jokes…

You tried the rugalach at the bakery by my house?
That place is serious.

It's just a tiny door, but enough to get scared.
Why do you mock my gloves?

§§§§

(*Your hair's gotten longer.*)
I was thinking of getting it trimmed,
But I was also thinking of just getting it shaved again,
But then
(*You weren't happy with it the last time.*)
But I thought I was.
It ended up all right.
Now I look back on it fondly.
The short really does look good on you.
I'm just going to get a trim dude.
So, you know, when you go to the hairstylist
Can you tell them
"Make it the same except shorter?"
Because it occurred to me that it might be the type of thing

You think makes sense,

But then because they know what actually needs to happen

It doesn't.

(One of the weird things, especially with guy's hair,

Is that you mainly need the back cut

Because your hair shouldn't actually be the same length.)

§§§§

Think I thought about the fact that you liked it

last time I saw it

in the National Gallery,

all patriotic, exemplifying our heritage

or our purchasing power

owning all the great art after crushing Europe.

They've been bad for a couple of years.

The Rams never retooled since they were good,

so fast and everything was so exciting

with all their crazy offensive moves

and then a couple of their best players

fell out of their prime,

lost a step, fell apart; so you can't really get that into them.

But you can always root against the Patriots on the DL.

You mean, you're not going to go into a bar

and pronounce your hatred of the Patriots?

I don't have any ability to watch sports.

You would never watch it by yourself at the crib?

I couldn't understand it.

That's why being in a bar is great,

people just start explaining it to you

when you have that blank expression.

Football seems especially confusing.

That's what it seems like from

the ways girls talk,

understand the least.

But you just sort of have to like it.
It's not like you're going to be like
    ohh that's what happens on third down,
    now I like it.

§§§§

Watched *Breakfast at Tiffany's*, but didn't finish.
Audrey Hepburn is so graceful and hip. Did something weird happen
in the end? It's not even like she's a great actress. Well,
you don't even think about it. When do you think people stopped
talking like that, with that weird English accent?
I bet that's what New Wave movies did.
But I think well-bred people actually talked like that,
I'm not saying that it was just an invention of the movie.

Maybe the same reason why the '60s seemed so violent,
like my grandmother's hatred of
the fact that my mom liked Bob Dylan,
a fact that is totally unimaginable today.
    What, that she loved Bob Dylan?
    No, that my grandmother hated it.
Unimaginable,
    like Grace Kelly in *Rear Window*, really fuckin' cool,
    goes out with this cool guy, all proper;
    okay *Roman Holiday*, she's a princess, and you know
    as soon as you see her gorgeous foot
    you say *this is a great movie and this a cool chick.*
I would venture to say that chicks like that are cooler than chicks now
    who do whatever they want
    and everyone's a cool chick,
    but I'm saying that cool chicks will arise,

1: p50 · 2

their spirit is not going to be ruined by these institutions
    how is this possible with restraint and constraints
and that people are relatively interesting
    by nature…

but people don't exist for you to be entertained

well, yeah, right, so why is everyone so interested in being interesting?
    a reactionary argument,
        not such an argument for why things weren't so bad
        because people don't exist for you
    but that doesn't change whether or not they would be interesting
    so it's not an argument against my argument; it's immaterial what I want
        it's just saying that your argument is not an argument;
            the reason that certain institutions aren't phat for women
            doesn't have to do with whether they
            make women more interesting
    but that's what I'm wondering, saying, asking…
            because being unique and interesting is so important, and
            because conformity is such a threat that people feel
            that being interesting is essential to people
            and that is one of the reasons why people think
            cultural restraints are bad;
                what I'm saying is that the argument
                doesn't go through
                because the lack of constraints
                doesn't make people remarkable
then people will move back to them of their own accord
    people don't stop getting married,
    they don't stop going to church   *1*
            but they do all those things less;
            hard to imagine those institutions
            sustaining themselves
                unless there's something
                very different about America.

§§§§

    …just bought a bunch of stuff to make pasta
        at home: oil, garlic, spinach;
  so much cheaper, to stay on top of it,

and my roommate started cooking again;
it'll just make it better to live there now,
because if it's just two people
who don't give a shit about anything
and who are content to sit in their rooms all day
it's not good for the house.

    He lost his car, you know?
    And he didn't get it back and I'm not sure
    if that means that he can just say
        "Okay, fine, you can have my car"
    and then it's all over,
    or if there's something he needs to do,
    and I've definitely noticed legal notices at home,
        but we don't talk about it much.

1: p100 • 1

I'm pretty sure getting your car foreclosed on
has to be one of the worst things for your credit.
    it's gotta be worse than the stuff I do.
What do you do?
    I don't pay my credit card bill.
Not even the minimum?
    not for like a year
Not even the minimum?
    no, I don't pay anything on it.

    And I still have some bills from before I moved.
    And then whenever I actually have enough money to pay them
    it doesn't seem worth it.
    And then when I want to pay them I realize I don't have enough money.

You gotta just pay the minimum.
    Yeah, but if you don't have any money
    you're not going to pay the minimum.
    What if you only have a couple hundred dollars?
    Are you going to pay your bills then?
    Well, you can pay the minimum and then still use the credit card.
    Ideally you're right, but now it's shut off.

I'll take care of it later, like when I'm a lawyer.
Once this life thing lets up then I'll be responsible.

mixture of policy, circumstance, and choice
and the phat thing he says is that   poor people's bad decisions
     are a lot more significant
     and their good decisions   are a lot less…

I'm lucky because my panic doesn't concern spirit, but substance:
I'm just an alcoholic.   *1: p92 • 2*
Whenever I drink I just want more
and all my bad panicky memories are filled with alcohol.

I just kick it straight up American style.
I live way beyond my means, accrue a lot of debt.

I don't understand how you know that about yourself.
Because you don't think it'll happen again.
Why did I buy all this stupid shit?
Why did I drink so much and act like an ass?   *2: p9 • 2*
People know all sorts of shit.

But then, people do change.
    Maybe that's only on TV.
I think some crazy shit happens and people come out of it different.
    I'm just not sure that you can decide of your own free will to change.
    But you could decide to create an intervention.
    Like rehab, you only have to use your willpower for a second,   *3*
    and then the rest of it is against your will.

    §§§§

that makes sense as a juxtaposition, right?   *4*
    right
so you have these classical philosophers versus the law
and then you have Christianity versus the law,

but Christianity isn't just for Jews,
        not just a critique of the Jewish law…

the critique becomes universal

           scraping
        under,

the main question becomes
does Christianity make people feel as if they're chaffing under any law?

           against law
             as such

both of which it's fighting against;
        isn't that fucking money in the bank?
because for us custom means nothing
but for the ancients it meant everything
and it meant that if you broke a custom you were alone,

1   *and now, all we want is to be alone,*
                  feeling tradition differently now
and the way ritual has changed
has changed our idea of custom
        and that if you felt in yourself that you didn't want to follow a custom you would have to
        explain that.

                §§§§

2   but banishment isn't an element of brainwashing
        well, yeah it is, the threat of banishment, the threat of being alone
the threat of it is, but not the actual banishment
3: p229 • 2   *well fine, the threat is the custom, the prospect of reward and punishment*
but customs aren't totally objectified to us
        the prospect of banishment feels different to us than it would of to them
you're saying you would feel like you were banished if you didn't follow a custom
        no you would be banished if you didn't follow a custom

there's nothing more real than using language but people have always changed   1: p7 • 1
language

       we assume language as fixed
       but don't expect
       that when we use it incorrectly
       we'll be exiled

we still might be banished for saying the wrong thing:
       any college professor right now could say that
       black people are stupid
and be pretty fucked up

or they could say that
women have no place in our philosophy department
       and tell me whether or not they would be banished?

and before that the highest level
was marked by people
who thought that the law wasn't enough.

doesn't Jesus still think that the law isn't enough?
somebody on the West Wing thinks that the law isn't enough.
that's the thing, most people are in contradiction with themselves
       the negative would be that
       they think that the law is oppressive in that it
                      cramps their style
       they think it's not enough
               because President Bush
               is stomping on the Constitution.   2: p136 • 2

But this is completely uninteresting psychologically:
       it's just that we all want the law
       to apply to everyone else
       but not to us,
it's just a really watered down version of wanting to be a tyrant.   3: p178 • 1

§§§§

here's my gaffle
    (you mind if I gaffle you for a little while?):

      Shakespeare is a nihilist, but what kind of nihilist?

all of Shakespeare's plays are problem plays
none true comedies
none true tragedies

    the comedies are problems
    because political rulers
    are the means by which everything is resolved
        (Theseus in *Midsummer Night's Dream*,
        the Duke in *Measure for Measure*)
because what makes the comedies comedic
is revealed to be within the hand of the poet,
not within the forces driving the characters —
    the marriages, the resolutions,
    would not take place
    without some sort of deus ex machina —
(the duke doesn't have to kill himself)
      but it's just these weird twists of fate
      that turn these comedies from tragedies —
    all of the comedies would be tragedies
    if they just played out naturally…

    afterwards exuded
      the second part
        of the argument,
          equally compelling…

1: p178 • 8

§§§§

is going to live a tortured marriage
play within the play
the image of her with another man
but knows she hasn't
but thought she did for such a long time
but it was a setup, a play, a fake can be explained
but he experienced the shock of thinking that she did
I don't think that's right, he knows she hasn't
what you see isn't erased by what you know; the characters cared
that wasn't what I was saying
but that's an extreme version of what you were saying
but I wanted it to be meaningful without the context of the characters   *1: p159 • 1*
which maybe it's not
which maybe it's not, which is the thing.

§§§§

outlined chance event
because Socrates was real and Plato was real
philosophers exist
and then there are,
like,
tyrants

between the true lawgiver and the moderate tyrant
still has that deep deep lust for power
but that sort of chance meeting hasn't occurred…
and if man can change
that means he can change from what he was
then man can change into something that no longer produces greatness

       this herd animal

       with an instinct for preservation

dominates

dominates

and dominates

       then there won't be any more individuals

         and we'll just blink and smile

           and say that we have invented happiness

             and it will be the reign of the last men

              and man will set like the sun…

PICAYUNE

He smoked the kind of cigarette that killed you—the strongest one in the world. How could this *1* document, apparently entitled "How to Make a Martial Arts Porno Movie," have come to him? It seemed more a polemic expressing the need for such a film than a guide to making it. On the cigarette box, unironically, there was a picture of a sailor. He would watch a movie like that. He would like to see a movie like that although he would never, ever, tell anyone that out loud. A shred of tobacco was lodged in his throat. This document a xerox of an email that someone had printed out, the text full of grammatical and spelling errors, a work defined by its desperate strangeness. *2: p83 • 1*

Yeah yeah yeah, the King, trapped in his regal popular culture and unable to think or dope his way out. Yeah.

Need—everything was about need. Somewhere. Somehow. At some level. He was afraid too. He was afraid he was burning himself up, himself and his needs. But the needs were burning too. The needs were making him burn.

Was that it, then, to burn yourself up?

Pleasure, okay. Pleasure had some funny definitions. Some funny incarnations. He coughed—this tobacco burned like acid. Pleasure and the flesh—pleasures of the flesh. Why not do everything? What was the difference? Study kung fu, smoke cigarettes, be the King. The live King, of course, with the dead King dead. *3: p172 • 5*

He threw the cigarette end in the street. With no filter, it would decompose.

He was too old, too soft, too lazy to study kung fu. Worse, he as a kid had believed in kung fu, but now he no longer believed. The movie, sure, he'd watch the movie. In the movie, there'd be beautiful, exotic women skilled in sexual techniques and kung fu. He was not sure if he anymore believed in sexual techniques. Still, they were something to see.

He thought as he went back towards the building that he could leave soon. Leave and go home and drink some whiskey. Try to forget his job and blot out his life.

He knew this was not the right way to think.

What about The Market? How was his attitude improving the performance of The Market? He was in The Market as everyone he knew was in The Market, and it was The Market that was the thing most likely to guarantee his future. There would not be a lot of use for kung fu or porno come Social Security time. There wouldn't be much use for Social Security either.

Didn't he realize that?

Like this six-page, small-font, single-spaced email meant anything: What was the intent? Somebody wanted to make the movie, let him make the movie, and the movie's made, and there's the movie. It didn't even seem American. This seemed like something from somewhere else like France. Like some Frenchman made this orgy of violence and orgy of orgies and then presents it like it means everything in the world.

That's the way it was.

He had to live with that. And with himself. Though he knew how burdensome he was. But this other apparently had no idea what a burden each one was to all those around him. And everybody else as bad, the loved ones as bad to us as we to them.

He couldn't stay in this doorway. He had to go back inside.

Everyone had to be somewhere, even this computer-crazed Frenchman, and he had to be here for a while yet.

Get his orgy on film. Send out his message. That'd put him on top. He'd have something then. That was the other, that was the other one's life.

He couldn't get that. Go back in, go back out, drink some whiskey. He knew it. He was settled. He was settled with his problems intact. But he had to go back in and appear, at least, to be making an effort. Always, always, always there was some going back. Even if there was nothing, if he had nothing to go back to, he was sure he would go back *mentally*. *Mentally*—that was the only true time travel.

With that he got the headache.

A quick headache, a pain at the front of his skull that lasted maybe a minute, maybe less.

Someone, he thought, had shot a beam into his skull.

Funny how he thought that. He did not believe that. It was just something floating around, something from the TV.

Regardless, he had to go back in for some more time.

Couldn't it just pass? Couldn't he just sit in there as though he were in a trance? Why not be in a trance? He saw himself as a man with a desire to be in a trance state. If he had that movie, and he put it in his VCR and watched it, he could sit there as though in a trance. He could watch it again and again.

But he might not be in a real, an authentic, trance. Why, he thought, was he denied a trance state? It wasn't part of his culture, true, but how long did he have to suffer at the unknowing, the uncaring, mercy of his culture?

What did he get? Instead of the trance states he got, what, the Promised Land? The problem with the Promised Land was that inescapable and unenforceable promise. Instead he got to go back inside and toil by the sweat of his brow. Or something like that.

Okay. Yeah, all right. He had this temp thing writing curriculum for inclusion in a software package. Right, right, right. He knew how to do it. He, he, he had been a teacher.

He should have brought some whiskey with him. You know, in a little flask. But that would be bad. He couldn't let himself do that. Just as he couldn't make or participate in the making of a martial arts porno movie. Wasn't in him. Wasn't who he was. Or could be. Prisoner of his culture, his idea, his ego, his head. Couldn't think his was out. Couldn't *feel* his way out.

1: p26 • 1

2

3: p177 • 9

4: p104 • 2

5: p170 • 1

6: p154 • 5

Somebody's, not his, escaping the ego. There was a trap to be sprung.

Nope. Not his.

Back to the Spook House, one way or the other. Earn his daily bread.

He knew a woman. Yeah, yup. She was brilliant then. Now she sold things or helped sell things. He had been a teacher. That was supposed to be better. Really he had helped people so they could be well prepared to buy things. To consume things like the movie. To take the movie, the stuff, the food, the cars—all—into themselves, in a way.

He took all that into himself. How could he not?

The best thing would be to live in a box.

But then—

The best thing would be to live in a box with her. He could be King then and reign with the Queen. Reign in this Kingdom of Junk.

1: p178 • 8

2: p158 • 2

3: p38 • 1

"PG. 24" A PSEUDO-LITANY,
BEING LINES WRITTEN BY ANON.

1: p52 • 1

2

3: p16 • 6

4: p197 • 1

5: p178 • 7

6

7: p196 • 1

8

9: p8 • 2

10

Rummaging through clutter, boxes & boxes strewn like flotsam or shipwreckage in one indissoluble heap, up in my fiancee's attic one snow-bound afternoon in Pigeon Cove, MA, I happened upon two shoeboxes of floppy disks & opened them, hoping to determine their owner, their origin, anything pertinent—the house, inherited from her great grandparents, at times seemed foreign territory she once shared, Platonically, with a strange man who paid his share of rent on time, and never made waves, never showed any interest, other than obligatory & cursory etiquette, in my fiancee's affairs. (Were the floppies his? the Litany? The books & books of poems I discovered, abandoned like old clothes?) Once I heard him pacing and mumbling, reciting something intense & powerful (rhythmic) to himself again & again, the words lost to the muffling of the wall between us. Had he thought we were conspiring against him? Clicking around the floppies, I discovered the following: page 24, scattered throughout several files, arranged in various configurations, and imagined it was his voice, so quiet and murmuring in my head as I perused each fragment, each line. An educated man, I have long felt responsible for their discovery, and here—previous iterations notwithstanding—have selected what I believe are each "composition's" definitive locution by (what I had found, merely fragments; the poet, unknown) our still unspoken "Anon.":

Stropt "elocutions / executions" (estranged words)
Mapped (neighborly?) in langue-repose. On pg. 24.

Whilst ammo.

A poem abridged.

Alliterates / obliterates civilizations
Spelled "oddlye" on pg. 24.   Pg. 24 attacks.

"Blank white page."

Aggressively w/ ack-ack aggressively.

Not of necessity but by virtue of its circumstance.
&by this it is meant on pg. 24:

Old Spice GermX Qtips Crest Tegrin Lancômbe are prose poems.

Bar codes.

Signs beside poetry's oval sink on pg. 24.

This is pg. 24.
This is pg. 24 the following day:

Pigeon Cove to Manassas to Point Reyes: Lisa driving lines across lines on pg. 24. Blue gift bags never vary by a single word. The hours ask dolor for color on pg. 24. There is hope equated with pg. 24. (There in the glare of the particulars stands Lisa holding a volume of Frost open to pg. 24. King off on woods in Trojan is tycoon.) The shoals being eastern is the crux of the matter on pg. 24. Pg. 24 & pg. 24 are identical to a point. But not in time.

1: p53 • 2

2: p150 • 2

DEAD LETTER GAME

1: p178 • 9

2

At times I got off on the collision of bad luck and good timing. Something feral, almost seductive, in the *conditions* of sportive engagement. The result, as the advertisement says, a kind of "electric diary" transmutable in accordance with weather, state of health, work schedule, and habits of conscious ordering.

3

For example, the order of actions was predictable, which made for an easy assessment of value. Meaning fell into the shelter of a long-term project. Value and meaning, thus conflated, had little if anything to do with the finished thing, the artifact. Always a vanquished meaning in this efficient use of mourning. A sense of flow and accretion, to be sure, a formal satisfaction. If not empty vessel, then the weight of the cup when thirsty.

4: p180 • 6

5

6: p173 • 2

Then, the always important follow-through, turning over (weight of deeds performed). Plus, the tendency to work in groups of three: first, the drone of experiment (improvisation); second, duplication of perceived measure (prisonhouse of habit); third, a managed resistance to failure (secondary duplication, in dead letters).

Dear Nadine,   *1*

                    I am so very sorry,
and regret very sincerely,
my long-delayed reply to your letter.
But let me begin:
I began the poem in question
as a sonnet: 14 lines (Petrachean:
abbaabba, cdecde.)
It's now an epic-postmodern,
its own lyric-agonistes. I excerpt
page 24 here as penance:

            In terms oceanic pulses.

            / directly similar: In part denizens
            —coral'd & banded,

            perfect in symmetry!

But yes, Nadine, writing
is but speaking's other
stratagem. Not to be tread upon.
It senses. It wriggles
with wind to fit / to find
one more instance of itself
in order to cohere.
Having neither sepals.
Nor formidable aspect.
But song—
one white Amur [ashen] & [lilac].
                    Best wishes,
your contrite
& tardy correspondent.   *2: 157 • 3*

STILL

1: p16 • 4   situational, room is only room. perhaps
                 this is only the best. perhaps this noise
2: p152 • 6   the furthest from truth.

3: p102 • 2   if in fact there is noise.

                 this corner of somerset harbours holes in
                 the ground, a small plastic duck. the
4: p67 • 8   water remembers the shape of the stone.

5: p191 • 1   if a crushed language leaps. if chalk rolls
                 through the window or still.

LOST LANGUAGES

Development of language on open plain: *1*

    relationship with horses?   *2: p193 • 1*

    Linguist himself entombed in North Stacks of library—a tiny carrel,   *3*
with half a window open to the street. A secret garden, this small stretch   *4: p35 • 1*
of gray steel and tan linoleum. Half a street vendor visible—back of head,
one shoulder, torso and thigh wrapped in apron. Vendor starts fire. Roasts
potatoes. Librarians 20 years ago removed from carrels all protrusions that
could be used for attaching a noose.

Barriers to communication—

    extant writings refer only to unpleasant or mundane

        -laws safeguarding privileges of parasitic priestly class   *5: p17 • 1*
        -edicts against trespassers
        -a log of trades in purple-dyed wool

JOURNAL ENTRY: 12-26-05

Seeking seed texts in <u>Gravity's Rainbow</u>
Concise airraiding of textual anomalies the id vs. postmodern gestalt.
Re: pg. 24: <u>A Writer's Reference</u>:
"Are ideas ordered effectively? Is the supporting material persuasive?"

[Was T.P., I wonder,
utilized by order his words intended to deconstruct?

A snuff box of self?
An object half structured as language is half structured?
It is precisely 7:08 a. m. in N. Y.
T. P. ponders what wld happen if
a screaming came twice, murdering, out of the same sky.
Then writes anonymous horoscopes aloud in the observatory while looking up.
His cat is pearl-eyed & Persian.
What does time have to do with

ash-of-the-makebelieve people falling in september?
In the loom room he wends his wangled word-way.
Cold War enigma-hardon "is both organizer & destroyer" of nothing.
Yet desires to devour
considers its HEALTH, its few DOLLARS,
riffles, yet precisely, snug in QUOTES paid for on credit,

LAZY BOY recliner,

MIDDLE CLASS as only [here I need something strong]
POST-WAR AMERICAN MALE can be,

& thinks, Yeah. Let there be WORD PLAY
& ESPIONAGE/espionage
& PORN straight out of SODDOM,

that thunka thunka thunka of bed legs
pounding the floor, even if only imagined.
The left hand, the writing hand, poised as a pilot's,   *1*
crazed as a hanging judge's,
"is both organizer and destroyer."
His rapture, dolled up in genocide,
can only imagine pg. 24 buried in text.
A piece of writing breaking ground.

I can't help but feel…I keep imagining…I have this sense that T. P. is listening
at keyholes, that what I write unravels to paraphrase no matter what I write.

DEAD LETTER GAME

1: p172 • 6   I no longer use source text because I trust neither source nor text. A source is too slippery, volatile. You never know where the next one will burst forth, and there's no telling who has put in before you. Text, that seeming neutral, blankets an old regime. You can almost hear it like a chorus of giddy and wine-drunk cherubs: *we love you*, they mutter dolefully, and the lie clings to every weave.

2   This near-diabolical reliance on metaphor pretty much makes the case. There must be better ways to organize (then pressurize) the activity of, what, wordcraft? Not quite, but at least to reconvene on the other side of this experiment, active since Mallarmé, by which the materiality of signs has
3   come to stand in for the *kinderwurk* of an able if unschooled group of aspirants.

The world today at all of its fixed portals (ways and means of multiple, numbered worlds)
4: p195 • 12   communicates its losses sometimes faster than the losses themselves. The cry of the burn victim in the aftermath of bombing rebounds absurdly, strikes distant listeners as an afterthought. Perception is key, and worlds collide, disintegrate, recombine in the narrow spaces between one's
5: p170 • 1   ordinary bouts with vision.

So, we can willfully buy into this faster-than-light self-immolation (a body, so to speak, turning inside out in an effort to catch itself winking) or we can opt out. I'm not sure this is a real choice,
6: p1 • 6   but there are commitments to be made all the same.

PROPERTIES

The mask. The mask may not inflate, though blood is flowing to the mask. Please secure your own mask before masking the consanguineous. Your eyes will blood-blind, do not be alarmed. Blood will spill over your breasts as you gag foolishly against drowning. Do not be alarmed. Simply compel the consanguineous to rub the viscosity into your flesh, paying particular attention to the porous nipples. Take him by the hand. He will oblige; the blood you share seeping under his torn hangnails as he guides it down toward the doorway of his one-time home. You feel it like a knocking. Do not be alarmed. Open the flooded airlock. The bends of shared blood bubble through you; champagne-like sensory failure. The labyrinthitis of the world.

1

2: p24 • 1

ESQUISSE

1   There's a terrific, and terrifying, passage in Gerhard Roth's *Will to Sickness* that captures what I am attempting in serving as your guide from shame to excess. "As she walked, the girl pulled her skin over her head, a long bloody sheet, and stood in glittering splendor in the gutter." What I want is nothing less than for excess to strip off your skin (not to mention my own), to leave you standing, bare and exposed, blood and flux and nerve and bone, in glittering splendor, a figure from a Francis Bacon painting.

2   But it is more complicated than this, for, to steal the words of another friend, *You will never know to the very end if I was laughing at you*. I have, you know now, asked you to lose yourself in excess, to abandon any notion of self, and yet to also remain painfully self-conscious, to never forget you

3: p25 • 1   might be the subject of a joke.

4   Such a paradoxical vacillation between self-dissolution and intensive self-consciousness is the

5: p211 • 1   crux of my tutelage. It is not unlike the way de Sade's characters sometimes insist that God doesn't exist and then in the next breath shove tiny copies of the Lord's Prayer up each other's anuses as a way of insulting God. They want it (and in fact get it) both ways: *God doesn't exist and yet we must insult him*. Or for us: *You don't exist: don't you forget it*.

Where does this leave you? In a fix. Neither coming nor going, simultaneously in anguish and

6: p28 • 3   ecstasy—which is precisely where I want you. There's real breathless power in this disjunctive synthesis, in the non-coincidence but simultaneity of anguish and ecstacy, of the certainty that

7: p22 • 1   God doesn't exist and the erotism of profanation, of the self and non-self.

All of which is tenuously but intensely connected to another passage, one I find equally terrifying, this one from Yoel Hoffmann: "Sometimes the bell rang and a person we did not know

8   stood in the doorway. I am so and so, he said, and have no hand. But he *had* a hand."

What makes the passage so terrifying is the emphasis it places on that last *had*, a desperate insistence that reveals not the narrator's logical certainty that a hand was there, but his uncertainty and the utter void of his fear.

9   Is not this void at the bottom of all that we attempt, be we mother and son, lover and lover, or writer and reader?

PROPERTIES

The dress. The dress undresses itself. Those buttons running up the back are bone. They pop 1
off, roll across the floor in search of their body. Follow them. The bone corset-stays writhe
free and slide down your thighs fingerlike. Crawl to catch them. The leather strap unbuckling,
bucking against its stitching. Your hands grasp for cloth yet find only flesh, yours. Unseamed,
unseemly, you are open on your hands and knees. Behind you the flesh red dress rises, its button
eyes of the dead.   2: p98 • 1

femina, fex Sathanae, rosa fetens

1: p40 • 4

in the laboratory lie women, moist and humid, vulvas weeping.

2: p172 • 1

    machines collect the secretions—scraping and exsiccating uterine walls, extracting fluid from sexes dank as caves. basins fill to the brim with the brackish runoff. tears and urine. milky flowings. bloody sweats. sexes blooming like a field of fetid roses. plucked. *les fleurs du mal, les flueurs blanches*. the laboratory is lined with steel receptacles. tubs in which women have soaked for months, bodies softening until the membranous parts, like parchment, have dissolved, detached—exiting the body through the bladder, excreted through the pores of the flesh. the women's bodies exuding, effluvial. like sirens submerged. each tub an ocean. each body aquatic. at night, the scientists use a system

3

of weights and pulleys to winch each woman out of the water. dredging the defluent bodies from their immersions, exhuming them for brief inspections. the scientists test the suppleness of the women's skin, prying back the peeling layers. their hands part the women's thighs. searching for something solid, some internal substance that will not deliquesce. the women suspended above the water, ponderous and dripping. sirens surfacing to air. the scientists, like sailors, nestled between

4: p28 • 1

their knees—bowed before, amidst, below that wet shrine.

AND YOUR MESSAGES

read, They are starving us, or, They have cut off my ears, or, They have pierced my   1: p92 • 1
eyes, or, They have cut off my hands. And you wanted to cut off my hands. You told   2
me the gangrene would set. And I was the woman who fingered her necklace, having   3
admitted to having a dream. Then you cut off my hands and told me I couldn't vote
for democracy. You said, Go to the olive tree. But I'd cut off my hands just to touch   4: p234 • 2
you. Shut my eyes with dull wire. Tear out my heart so you'd know how I feel. Because
this is too big. You see it too clearly. This is too big. God refused to save me. And when
I steamed off the stamp, I found your hidden messages. And your messages read, They
have plucked out my teeth, or, They have cut out my tongue, or, They cut off my cuffs
and gave me a system. But your words were like blinds. So I asked you, Why I should
love this body? And you said, Because it is lordly. And I said, Should I prove false or   5: p17 • 1
weaken in my determination, may the soldiers of the Pope cut off my hands and feet.
So I cut off my hands and held them away and you said, Pull my hands and make them   6
yours. So I pushed my dead hands against your dead chest in hopes that I could serve
you. Trains slammed into one another. I tried to pull you out of the ditch, but the head
is always the longest journey. My body is still forming. My hands are still haunting. And
when you gagged my mouth, I sang through the holes of my eyes. I am yours only in
the dark. And you cut off my hands, sealed my ears with wax, sewed my mouth closed,   7: p18 • 2
and made my cords two twisted voids. Toilet bowl finger tuck voice box chain-gang. I
am sorry for your infatuation. I am sorry that you failed at the jail. I am sorry that you
carve the infinite shit. After all, the lost orchid isn't worth anything. So cut off my hands,
rational man, and hang me from the gibbet upside-down. The sky is all blown like a
scrap of paper. Because this is too big. And I don't care if it is the next big thing.

IT IS WRONG

1: p111 • 2 It is wrong said the ghost
to be astonished at anything

as everything is the same
given the right light

2 and sometimes the ghost
steps out from behind a tree

and the wolves go away

She sat at the edge of the playground, next to the swings, and finished the story:

"The bird flew up into the rafters
and landed there
looking almost natural

Sometimes a forest replaces the house
but it should not be confused with the children

3: p94 • 1 and the ghost should not be taken for snow, though
he will tell you, that is not what I meant
to do to you.

SING/LE FIGURE

Saw-edged scarf

A tear or mole, or mole so firm: haired

Whittling the quill that draws: flight

Now I'm your tears   *1: p170 • 2*

*

A group of figures is also a single figure, moving   *2: p10 • 3*

As alone sleep is insomnia

*

As the opposite of grass is not *not-grass* but also not *anything*

Loose-leaf jowls

Port city

*

Or: city port

Christ in Wood with Traces

Now I'm your bridge of trysts

The damned, with eyes, and everything   *3: p176 • 2*

FIGURES FOR A DARKROOM VOICE

1: p100 • 1

So this is what it means to pull an all-nighter from what forms the whispering in your kitchen cupboards. The police radio's comforting dispatcher ignores the private detective's stony leer & the minute hand badgers the waltz leader's epilepsy from the doorbell into his dog's notion of a spotting scope's dutiful mistress. We lift off a luster & carve a miniature elephant onto the doorknob. Background blending with foreground

2: p171 • 1

to prefigure perspective in an etching that resembles a water ode but sounds like a helicopter blade hacking apart a radio tower.

DEAD LETTER GAME

The disjunctive text has its charms, but you have to admit it may not work well in weak economies, under conditions of suspect leadership, especially. It's hard enough to know why the incense trail spirals the way it does, let alone why currents flow not this way but that. In other words, opacity haunts in the background, so why trouble the issue with evermore sleights of hand. There are other ways to provoke a mood swing, and really that's what writing is all about anyway.

1: p135 • 1
2: p156 • 4

The question of right practice cannot be severed from one's choices with regard to medium and mode. Here, a nod to the form/content dyad, but an added sense that practice as performance aligns differently with content. I move with a game piece, decide on a course limited by options determined by the current arrangement of other pieces and the board's configuration overall. I cannot reselect either the game piece or my available options. Making a move (form as performance) is very much *about* making that very move (content). Moving into (or toward) a new arrangement (setting, set of relations, context) touches or combines with that arrangement *as it goes*.

3

A bloody mess, I know, but nothing like the one I'm about to get into.

POST-HOLING TO THE FLESH TEMPLE

1   My physics professor, Dr. Slatoris, was being convicted of a crime against reality. He held an impromptu conference to counsel us students. After all, physics was the basis of our beliefs and without Dr. Slatoris we had no other direction to turn. The conference was held at a kibbutz/retreat fashioned after a Hindu temple in Aspen, Colorado.

    After dropping my bags off in my private bungalow, I ventured to the massive banquet room.

2   Most of the other students were high school delinquents. One freshman girl with ripped fishnet stockings was sobbing quietly to herself. Dr. Slatoris didn't waste any time. He filed down each

3   row questioning and consoling the students. He shielded himself with a plastic bubble that gave him a warped appearance so we couldn't identify him, which was ridiculous because we all knew who he was. The questions he asked were vague moral and ethical questions that didn't relate to

4: p232 • 1   the specific crime he had committed.

    "You don't seem very affected by what you did," I found myself blurting out.

    "You don't think I have regrets?" he yelled through his voice scrambler. "Observe!"

5: p196 • 2   He took a pair of scissors and started stabbing holes in the blackboard. Even the freshman in the ripped fishnet stockings stopped her sobbing. Dr. Slatoris picked up some chalk and connected the holes with spiraling arcs, segueing into a particle physics problem (see *Exhibit K*). His handwriting was messy and he was doing a lot of hand waving. Once again, we were distracted from the issue of why he was on trial. I wasn't knowledgeable enough about his case to put him on the stand, so I just took notes and re-sketched what he said.

    To distract us further and provide entertainment during our scheduled break, a heavy metal

6   band named *Platinum Blonde* was setting up. The guitarist was going through a sound check with a hollow body guitar that sounded tinny. They spent a long time warming up and getting everything set just right, and then never played anything when the time came.

7: p75 • 9   We got bored of standing around, so me and this guy Rig decided to take a walk along nearby Snowmass Lake. I left my shoes inside thinking we weren't going far. It felt good to walk barefoot on the pine needles. Once we left, a few others decided to follow us. Rig led the way at first. He was having troubles getting around the shore because he didn't want to get his shoes wet. It didn't matter to me that my feet got wet. I used the hanging tree branches for balance. Rig followed. It was getting muddy under the surface and I started sinking. Everyone including Dr. Slatoris was back on the shore watching. It got to the point where the water was above our private parts.

8   The lake got deeper and sludgier, turning to putrid oil. The bottom was scummy quicksand. We pushed our bodies through the muck, with our hands reaching to the sky for balance.

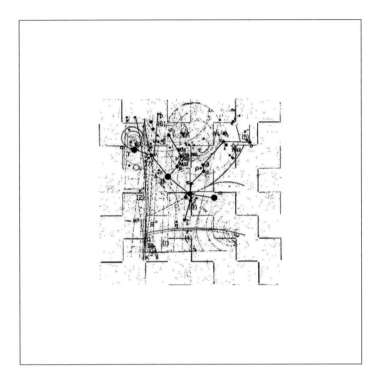

Exhibit K. The Collision

1: p154 • 1

There was nothing to derive momentum from. Cliffs were caving in around the edges. The water was bubbling and boiling even though it was freezing cold. The shoreline tapered off vertically, but if we were part of that motion, then we could just as easily perceive it as a lack of event horizon. 2: p113 • 2

It made no sense to get pulled under, so I started to swim in the mucky molasses. I called 3 back to Rig, but he was reluctant to go in all the way. The "water" was getting denser and darker. Rig was yelling that we needed to find somewhere to hide. He was reading instructions from a 4: p100 • 2 cheat sheet, "it say's there's a cave, but do you trust Dr. Slatoris' judgment? It could be a trap." 5: p151 • 1

Out of the blue ether, something was stinging my body. There were fish shapes moving in the corner of my eyes—primordial swishes from dorsal fins and swooshing crocodile tails. I was beginning to get scared and had to remind myself, as I usually did when I found myself in situations like this, which was never, that the fear was all in my mind. I lifted my severed arm out of the water and what was left of it was covered with leeches. What I felt and saw didn't line up. I put my arm back under water and it felt fine, but crabs were biting my legs. I took a deep breath and concentrated on retaining my composure.

1   The "cave entrance" was on the surface of the water. If the level of the lake was one foot higher it would've spilled into and filled the cave. I climbed onto the edge of the entrance and the leeches slid right off, revealing my real limbs. Below the cave entrance was a huge vaulted room with magnificent columns in a state of decay. Even though they looked Romanesque, I assumed they were Hindu because they matched the architectural style of the kibbutz.

     From the rim of the cave entrance, I jumped on to a thin Formica tabletop that extended hundreds of feet on top of a very narrow pillar in the center of the vault. There was nowhere else to go. I realized I was there (our destination) and turned to call back to Rig. "I'm on top and there's no way down."

2   "How did you get to the top in the first place? You can't make it the top if you were never at the base." He was rotating the hand drawn map in different directions to get a fresh perspective. "These directions are sequential. They assume a singular starting point."

3   Below me, at the pastured base of the shaft, the mopey girl in ripped fishnet stockings was gazing up and wondering how I got there. A string of spittle was dripping from her mouth but she sucked it in before it dripped onto the lawn. She was jealous and scared, but worshipped me at the same time. This was empowering. I knew everyone's thoughts. I kicked a metal cotter pin off the ledge just to hear it hit the ground. Even as it fell, it sounded hollow. The ringing reverberated within my head. I couldn't know for sure what it sounded like to the others below and was not even sure it ever hit the grassy ground. The fishnet-stockings girl was scrambling over boulders to flee the temple. Only from her reaction could I tell it was all collapsing.

4   When this thought entered my head, the elevated platform started swaying. I started spinning clockwise. I wasn't sure if I was actually spinning or if I was just getting dizzy in my ears. My body leaned out over the edge so my eyes could check my relative motion in reference to the ground. The change in my angular momentum only made it worse. I couldn't help myself from being scared and knew I would fall as a consequence. I froze into suspension of disbelief and never fell.

     Breaking loose from my frozen state, I jumped and clung to the outer wall. There was also a tribe of monkeys casually hanging out on the sheer cliff face. It was difficult for me to hold on even though genetically we all came from a common ancestor. Then it occurred to me that the swaying shaft I was perched on was a monkey tail, and since it was white, I knew I was on the tail tip of Hanuman, the notorious white monkey from the Ramayana epic. But at the base of the pillar/tail was a giant chessboard, so then I realized that what I had been on top of was actually an exaggerated rook that was taller than all the other pieces on the board, even though the queen technically had the most power.

5   "You can't castle now!" Rig yelled up to me. "The king has already been moved."

     Dr. Slatoris appeared from behind the column to chime in that castling, like quantum tunneling, didn't make physical sense, but was just a construct of convenience.

6   Dr. Slatoris had been using us all of this time. Or rather, he was kibitzing a divine source we

7: p38 • 1   could not see. The girl in the fishnet stockings was his black queen. Rig and I were white rooks.

It was all becoming clear. By learning from him, we had become pawns in his crime. The kibbutz was a game board for his guilty pleasures that went against the grain of humanity. Through this unseen channel, he castled to force me to switch my strategy. Now that I was self-aware, I took over from where he left off and sat there for seven days and nights. I can't remember who won, but I remember feeling confident that I was but one piece in the process of surviving. This was all I could speak for. To this day, Dr. Slatoris (who is serving time) and I correspond by playing chess through the mail. He still has not confessed. I am serving out his sentence for him.

1

2: p133 • 1
3: p92 • 3

1: p221 • 1

Dear W,

The fur on the shoe made one imagine a deer a pig an animal as the inference with the woman—and the man who gave the shoe was what?

No Americans were hurt.

The movie trailer narratives, broken up pieces of the sequential film, were much more interesting than the film itself. Displaced sections, gestures, things put into different contexts by enjambment with the neighboring information.

2: p191 • 1

Basically, a nightmare.

NECK

stills into an inconvenient nightmare.   *1*
construction comes in jars. the only way
to leave this place is to deliberately lift.   *2: p151 • 1*

everything is gentrified. the peel of a taste
of skin over blue sky blue is a layer of
dust. the skin that would otherwise be.

I am hopelessly incomplete; I am   *3: p105 • 5*
hopeless and this. green car passes,
shakes; green car is the key to a pardon.

today I am human; thrum on its neck.   *4: p59 • 4*

DEAD LETTER GAME

Nearing play time. The pressure's on to *produce* (I blame only myself for that) but in a different, perhaps reformed, way.

But why different? What reform? I've been close to it for a while now, this hesitation to name the game for what it is: the issue, I mean, is hesitation, deferring the inevitable, equipment assessment as convenient distraction.

1: p152 • 2

But all is not lost: imagine vital alliances between the given record (these entries, as *proceedings*) and future endeavors perceived as fresh and unmarked, untainted. Maybe equipment has been there (available, ready) all along, and I have simply failed to pick it up and use it. More hesitation, distraction.

2: p174 • 1

The eyes of the dead stare out while closed lids shield us from that eventuality. These letters, a kind of shielding disguised as whimsy, preclude their own outcome. That's the best I can do, I'm afraid, to describe how the very act of playing can be its own equipment, its own arsenal against all forms of invasion, corruption, and competition (those life strategies requiring tactical responses).

3: p155 • 1

4

Let's put it this way, in italics: the letter-writer revisits his own letters with a healthier attitude. I have "come out in the wash," so to speak, and am therefore equipped, i.e. ready, *for anything*.

THE KING AND THE COTTER PIN

> I kicked a metal cotter pin off the ledge just to hear it hit the ground. Even as it fell, it sounded hollow. The ringing reverberated within my head.
>
> —*Derek White*, Post-Holing to the Flesh Temple

I delivered Slatoris his groceries. When? December, 2005. I was a young man waiting for something to happen. There was, I remember, snow all that winter. I looked for any excuse to stay awhile to get warm.

He liked to play chess. He wasn't much good at it, though he thought of himself as a master of the game – of strategy. I could have beaten him easily, but what would have been the point? He would pour me a drink (he liked gin) and, pointing to the board on which he had overnight made a move to counter my last, one for himself. A large one, with bitters. We played every day – each day a single move. Every morning he'd call up with an order – what he needed for the afternoon and night and next day's breakfast. So I had – you see – to come each day, up the fire escape (he was afraid of fire and always took a room, if it were on the third floor or above, next to one), with a bag of – I cannot remember now what it was he ate. Except the cookies. Kings, they were called – shortbreads robed in Belgium chocolate, filled with raspberry cream. I picked them up for him at Teak's. The girl had given him his first taste of one – the girl with the ripped fishnet stockings. I brought him his gin, too. Gordon's. He liked me to "arrive by the fire escape"; he liked – he said – "a dramatic entrance."

He also liked to talk. By then, he was an old man – at least so he seemed to me, who was just twenty-two … twenty-three? Twenty-two that winter – just. I don't think he had anyone else to talk to. It was all behind him – his life, his life's work. Whatever it was that was his work; I hardly understood it at all. He said he didn't need anyone; his mind – he said – was "sufficient." It projected onto the world everything there was, "like a Magic Lantern." He was – he said – "at the center of all there is." Even me. "You are my own creation," he once told me: "my own self's interlocutor. My very own End Man." I did not understand half of what he said to me. He said, "I will make of my imagination a room and live in it." You could not say he drank too much. He was – his eyes were … they shone with – fanaticism. Rapture.

You want to know about the time he brought the school kids to Aspen to – I never could understand why he brought them there. A conference. He had been arraigned for a crime against reality.

1

2

3

4: p194 · 1

5: p193 · 5

6: p41 · 3

7: p38 · 1

8: p198 · 8

9

10: p16 · 5

He never said by whom. To talk about it was the only time I saw him laugh. Laughed so hard tears came to his eyes. You see he'd set the whole thing up, like a – you know he was a con man, right? No, that's not at all what he was. He was like P.T. Barnum – a showman, a producer of spectacles. That's how he put it: "A producer of extravagant spectacles for an age that has ceased to be amazed by anything except its own smoke, its own sleight-of-hand." There was malice in it. In what he did. If you read Derek White's account of what happened at Snowmass Lake in Aspen – in the water and in the cave. (If it was water. It wasn't a cave – not a real one.)

Slatoris called himself a misanthrope – said he had managed to banish man and all his works. He replaced them with theater sets. "The world's a stage – my own," he said. The girl in the fishnet stockings – she wasn't real. Neither was the other boy, Rig. They were mechanical. He rigged them both – he rigged almost everything – even the pine needles the kids walked on from the kibbutz to the lake were bought from a theatrical supply house. Slatoris preferred mechanical things to electronics, loved player pianos and little tin toys you set going with a wind-up key.

White, the young man who seemed at the center of "My Aspen Subversion" (Slatoris called it) – the kid who nearly drowned in the muck and ended up on the cave wall with the monkeys – he wasn't real either. Nor were the monkeys. Not according to Slatoris. I asked him how White wrote a story about it all – a story Slatoris had given me to read – if he wasn't. Slatoris laughed and said stories are the least real things in the world – didn't I know that? Stories and writers, both. And what about the theatrical supply people – were they – what's the opposite of real? Replicas, imitations, facsimiles? I asked him why the girl's stockings were ripped if he had created her. "To show the necessity of imperfection, of disorder," he said. And the cookies? How did he explain them? He wouldn't. He smiled at me and ate one.

I admit the cotter pin was genius. To have made it – an old-fashioned mechanism, if you can call a penny's worth of bent, cheap metal a mechanism – to have made it out of iron instead of brass. That was genius.

I remember reading about it – about the Aspen subversion, his last – in some book. I was curious. The writer said it must have been – the cotter pin must have been made of one of the rarer metals, perhaps a metal known only to Slatoris. You see how he had conned them all? Was he, as he claimed, an expert in particle physics? No. Slatoris' drawing in White's story – "*Exhibit K: The Collision*" – was a map of the damp spots on his cellar floor after a California rain.

"It was a bit of iron wire," Slatoris said. "I knew it would rust and the whole damned thing would come crashing down. The genius was in the timing! I'd worked out failure with a book on structural engineering. I wanted the pin to give way just when the boy was up on the table – the giant chess table with the giant chess men – pure melodrama and *papier-mâché*! I'd built the cave, the chess pieces, the giant white monkey – all of it out of *papier-mâché* molded over wire armatures. It was my finest provocation – my most elegant subversion. My supreme assassination of the notion of reality. Reality! Reality is every man's to fashion for himself, if he once admits that there is nothing behind it, any of it – nothing. The cotter pin was genius! And the girl – I didn't give her a name. Even so, I fell in love with her – even if I'd made her and knew she wasn't real.

1: p144 • 2
2: p195 • 8
3: p171 • 3
4: p221 • 1
5: p191 • 4
6: p197 • 6
7: p213 • 3
8
9
10: p89 • 3
11: p197 • 3
12: p151 • 3

What was real – what is real? You" – he meant me – "do you imagine that you are real? Do you believe that this delicious King you bought me is real, or this excellent gin? Not even I am real – not even Dr. Slatoris! I'm waiting one day to look up from whatever I'm doing and see a cotter pin and, pulling it, bring down the world and be no more." That's what he said.

1: p154 • 1

One afternoon I came round the corner with a bag of groceries – end of winter, March – and the apartment building was gone. Slatoris'. Not burnt down or knocked down – gone, as if it had never been. Nothing left except an open box of broken Kings in the grass. Chocolate on my fingertips, raspberry cream at the corners of my mouth, I asked some people – shopkeepers, a mailman – but no one had ever seen the building ever. What's it mean? Christ if I know! But whenever I see a cotter pin lying around, I run like hell!

OPUS CALIFORNIUM

1: p152 • 8
Obsessed with pg. 24
of the record Gregor Mendel
kept of his experiments
in agri-alchemy-melancholia
(out west of vowels—1/2 text,
1/2 spawn—
mutating like cells
in a parked SUV),

2: p229 • 1
the grim padres of abominations
abandoned (too
soon) their quest for purer californium
(a protean element) / their flirtation
with substances
not occurring in nature—
i. e. purer californium.

3: p51 • 2
& damaged, & deranged,
by legacies of less than perfect progeny,
they analyzed cycles

4: p108 • 2
of their own inveterate defecation—
texture, aroma, size, time of day
but found only miscellanea
[c.f. pg. 24]
prophylactic as flesh

5: p112 • 2
aching thru morning's inexorable
mutations

un-   [progeny of isotopes]

stable.   (ImP erf-

6: p164 • 1
Ect.) etc. etc.—the experiment
posterity makes
of radiant darkness.

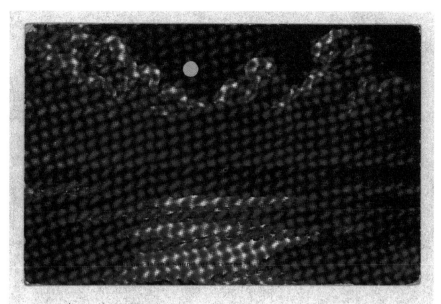

THIS MAGNIFICANT SCENE
PURPORTEDLY FROM A CENTURY
AGO COULD HAVE BEEN
REPLICATED EXACTLY IN
TEXTURE AND DETAIL FIFTY
YEARS LATER, SEVENTY-FIVE
YEARS LATER, AND EVEN NOW.

Richard Kostelanetz

1

2: p153 · 2

CATEGORY 5

1.

little baby beast

boy

sitting on concrete

eating skewered

meat

this is the way we are

were

have become

piling concrete upon a living being

crowding in front of bowery mission

clapping our hands for universal peace

waiting for the doors to open

this is how the view is

captured

built

the strafings

odd moments of clarity

bygones going by

yet not forgetting the residue

not collecting the residuals

these people

all want to give mew something

before i dies

then take it away.

2.

bush bush bush bush

bush bush bush bush

1: p145 • 2   bush bush bush bush

there i've said it. now hush.

3.

mush. slush. rush. flush.

4.

walking thru universe

wandering

grilled   skewered

distracted by menus   streetsigns & the moon

rollicking envy   gone 'fore you've arrived

captured   before   hatched

defrocked angels   lost little boys   waiting for the doors to open

searching for lost entrances

camouflaged   bullypulpits   creepy tactless oratories

amongst flat landscapes.

5.

4   3   2   1   ....   *1: p189 • 3*

STILL

This city

   is my relationship

touched by human hands
no one understands that

understands that when I take

     a picture

  but I do

take a step
the step you take
with you
on the bottom of your shoe

take the stairs

create the patina
placed by human hands

1   each brick   placed
               there is no machine for this

   yet

walk over the bullshit too

look in at empty lots
        MOTHER etched in the sidewalk
men play alley craps with
        lives

the abandoned
dilapidated

        she's not there

the shadows pass between
      buildings downtown
          a blimp appears

torn down

        by human hands
        weeds peek through

        rubble piles
        forgotten
        remains

marquee letters hanging
telephone *ringing*

        one side of the theater blown out

  ringing

a sports broadcast coming from an open window
through the screen and down the front stoop
decades ago

step over
the bull
shit

ringing

1: p158 • 3

how many rings does it take to topple a building?

just stop
wherever you are
lie down and go to sleep

or walk until you drop

what keeps some from this and not others?
to stop   to drop by

MY PLACE: Spanish & Italian Foods est. 1953
a line out the door

it comes down
            the buildings come down

            clouds come back

where does it go

the trash

how it is now

SEASON FINALE

My last look around the house   1: p68 • 2
took so long that the vine
climbing up the rosebush
beneath the bedroom window
climbed into my eyes,
and a lizard climbed, too,
mouthfirst from the grass,
skin changing color from grass-green
to a green almost without green,
the color of dust on feather.
How changed from last winter,
when the dog pawed the bed
and I let him into the yard
where we both whizzed
in moonlight, while rats ran
from the mimosa to the fence.
Small clouds pawed the galaxy.   2: p27 • 3
The shingles of the lawnmower shed
sparkled, and in the grass,
a cold lizard raised a claw.
Miraculous change,   3
but not enough to tell us
about the coming flood,
about the black line
the water would write   4: p156 • 4
as it rose along the plaster,
like a madman's scratches.
Safe in California, I'll hold
the cell phone hot against my ear
while in Louisiana my friend kicks
the back door in, and enters,

recording the damage
with the phone's camera,
and the images come through fast,
the bedroom window broken,
the rosebush ash-gray, the yard
ash-gray and without lizard.

FIGURES FOR A DARKROOM VOICE

wreck remembered film marks lifting a window   *1*

then enough is summer develop sounds apart full &

hinge a crown hive for lavender unlatched from   *2: p112 • 9*

otherwise winged & what refuses sheets a phantom   *3: p166 • 1*

story to marsh derailed from here   *4: p160 • 2*

regret botched glazing lugged sparrows a

constellation from apology fields exacted backward

keeps a finch & slows scenery borrowings

used as forwards on canticle a propeller

pitch missing & narrow might a building clown particulars

cracked behind becomes this garden camera & smoke

unbolts equals pulling points applause city improvisational   *5: p154 • 4*

a cloud landowner forgetting music inside

storm opening a crawlspace against & rusty an exit sign

FILM PROFESSOR WITH BEAUTIFUL HANDS

i am denied foremost by blankets—
by silos with ageing silver seed.
by the skins and edges of brain so flashing,

an ocular cult so brief, so remote

1: p108 • 3   as to demand that i carve a sliver-moon
into my hand:

a cipher cut for wolves
that speak in nascent tongues—who carry desire
in their vacuous mouths.

a celluloid click—pulsing red—opens
into the lens captured in the fist,
and the glyphs that float there:

2   the epistemic eyelid, the inutile buttocks of space-time,

3: p104 • 2   the bloom of yellow onto the humming gray screen, the flutter of a chamfered

4: p18 • 1   childhood. and then when two projectors stop

i am a limp bat affixed on the stiff suspension of a thick lens,
watched by slats and holes
rotating and winding parallel, halogen,
cross-teamed horses of light.

24

for example, turn more quickly than horses, horses more quickly than
stags, horn of a bull, hoof, half twelve, motion on tracks derives from the
more sensible realm of the sphere, such suchness itself, seeing him into and
out of, take the reality of the servant, for example, then paint a giant on a
pebble, you'll see that man is proportionate only to the fly, people here are
herding together to form all swarms of ants, back to the barracks, back
to the gurgling gunrest, the clouds are rising in the south, hens are rolling
in the dust, from this visible divinity, we can collectively presage rain,
concomitant, of course, with the kindling of flames, the ruin of all space,
shattered glass and toppling, from damp tamping of shadows, the divinity
of rain, one livid final flame, so the arrow is associated with the archer,
through narrow waters channels, the writer, of course, with the corpse

1: p105 • 3

2: p167 • 2

3: p27 • 3

4: p32 • 1 .

5: p16 • 1

6: p162 • 9

DEAD LETTER GAME

1   I got used to the idea of craftwork as strategic self-defense. I could never finish and so could never lose, or win. Practice, as rite, defined every moment of every day. Nothing escaped.

2: p152 • 5   Today I force back a grimace while reading through these records (the "electric diary" and other sources). No sense judging, even while the marks of discontent are obvious. The desire to self-incriminate (a kind of psychic house-cleaning) remains.

Informing assumptions included an unconditional faith in the power of language as intermediary, go-between, like the trussed effeminate body (medium) receiving spirits on behalf of a small group of anxious, hyperventilating live ones. The trips and false starts (muco-seminal dribblings) of an ear-bent consciousness would lead the way, find the channel, and in the wake of this experience an attendant flesh-node (me) could lean back and *be impressed*.

3: p157 • 1   The work was scholarly in its effort to mine the research moment. A kind of "reading," sure, but more the ruse of eliciting perception "nuggets," later told true in the imprint, the finished sequence. I see it now as bullshit but that's hardly the point.

4: p147 • 1   Playing this game is like scanning an old yearbook: the faces rise up afresh but as they have always been, secure and encrypted, perfect little corpses.

COMPOSITION 24

Place

A mug / A mask / Marbled / Apples / Ash / The blue / Twilled cloth /
Called Corpse / A horse / Before / A storm / To warn

Weathervane / Lodged torn in / The hedge maze / Days before /
At the first / Hint of I / Scry fruit trestled / As nave's ribs

Gunners on a / Courthouse roof the / Field sown with sweat /
Catching net set / Over fallen / Birds from wet wires

Tires chewing windchimes / Stole sills from under pies /
Painted carrier doves / On walls and struck as sets

Stet: let it stand I've made my peace / With birds interred in
south-shipped fruit / Then in skirt-slips warmed, singing out:

So, song is our only home (I'm: Hopscotch Chalk Corpse) /
How much loss until the first loss looks like love?

(I'm: *Closing Your Eyes in Claustrophobic Rooms Should Be No
Different From Closing Your Eyes in Meadows*)

1
2: p193 • 1
3: p110 • 4
4
5: p65 • 1
6
7
8: p169 • 3
9
10: p97 • 2
11: p54 • 2
12

1: *p197 • 4*

(...) _____ , _____ . { .... . } + { .... . } ____ ! (...)
(...) + { .... . } _____ , _____ . (...) ____ ! { .... . }
{ .... . } _____ , _____ . (...) + { .... . } ____ ! (...)
(...) ____ ! { .... . } + { .... . } _____ , _____ . (...)
(...) _____ , _____ . { .... . } + { .... . } ____ ! (...)

2: *p178 • 9*

(...) + { .... . } _____ , _____ . (...) ____ ! { .... . }
{ .... . } _____ , _____ . (...) + { .... . } ____ ! (...)
(...) ____ ! { .... . } + { .... . } _____ , _____ . (...)
(...) _____ , _____ . { .... . } + { .... . } ____ ! (...)

3: *p172 • 2*

(...) + { .... . } _____ , _____ . (...) ____ ! { .... . }
{ .... . } _____ , _____ . (...) + { .... . } ____ ! (...)
(...) ____ ! { .... . } + { .... . } _____ , _____ . (...)

DEAD LETTER GAME

The habit of repetition is the first object: that pattern of threes, for example, but other strategies emerged too, the worst requiring an exhaustive self-emulation to the point of emotional breakdown. And often some cataclysmic event was required to break the spell, or I'd go on in some mode indefinitely, convinced that I had cracked the code when really I had simply found yet another way to rally behind old habits dying hard.

1

2: p51 • 2

3: p185 • 1

4: p196 • 2

5: p112 • 3

One must practice, true, but things went wrong when the object disappeared behind a series of rote duplications. Copies of copies of copies, ad inf., until the illness came or someone knocked on the door.

6

7: p152 • 6

Which brings me to the second object: *love*.

8: p178 • 12

It's rather embarrassing, but I have to ask: When young, how else begin? What else motivates so readily? Death, maybe, but not with so many bills to pay. Love is cheap, or rather easy to please, and for a while it makes the game worth playing.

True, winning in most games is the object, but love is the object worth winning for. When this game finally turns over (as promised), I'll find a way to love it and maybe you will too.

Love repeated; repetitious loves; love's repetitions, etc. This game recreates (does not repeat!) the patience with which I lived out those days, in love and repetition, always on the lookout for the next good move.

23:59

What said and the response does not repeat itself
            but speaks as an immigrant/emigre softer
remembering Tuesdays with one marrying's *what*

and then she wept as I considered sandwiches
            with french toast from the french toast dispensing napkin
1: p112 • 6   dispenser I made everything with the french press

2: p52 • 4   started each sentence *O* for a time photographed
            anything and titled it *Place* the odd prices
3: p228 • 1   set so with tax to an even dollar *hotel*

before the hotel name at the *Hotel Before*
            we showered three times not *meteoric*, nights, but
meteoritic this language we could translate

4: p177 • 3   but not explain as turning a chessboard around
5   halfway through we traded lobster for lamb concrete
6: p67 • 5   split like marble still said *crack open a cold one*

opening each banana thus some happiness
            outlasts us average house size grew bottles' water
the only water the warning-planes light blinking

on towers because a steady draws (?) J.'s book-length
            on Pound then remembering Cafe Allegro
discussing how the rhythm leans at once forward,

7   back, because of photographs (mirrors, beds) it is
            easier for us to see beauty still today
8: p105 • 2   is my twenty-fourth birthday your dresses hang like

9: p98 • 7   a felled-tree's leaves...

2 4

oh k we make out that our privates sound as privates   1: p65 • 1
put on k we make out a single private in the morning
put on k seeing and catching deceive us
say seeing and catching sound like making out and hearing
he tears paper, she pushes in an open cap, but why "annoyingly"?

the essence is to look at the sword
the sword sees without thinking
the sword sees when it saw itself
and doesn't think when it saw
nor sees when it dresses its wound
the birds don't come for seeds
stop thinking already
let's make out   2: p56 • 2

but this (sad we cover our privates)
this exigence should be studied, deeply
an apprenticeship of forgetting
to hijack liberties of that convent
where poets write "stars sound as old old nuns"
with "flowers penitent convicts of the day"   3: p85 • 2
but on a final day stars sound as stars
flowers as flowers
privates as privates
which is why elas
we call to them
stars
flowers
swords
still, no birds
just a lot of
muxoxo

STUDENTS

PASSION

He was the kid whose story about kissing a girl made the rest of us quake, trying to hold in our laughter. I had to think of funerals in order to restore the class to a more suitable demeanor. We called him Menelaus because he had orange hair.

A few days later he was seen carrying the wildflower book. If we'd watched when he opened it, we'd have seen his finger on the hallucinogen *mandragora*.

That spring, the leaves were unusually large and soft. I imagine his fingers staining yellow as he pulled the berries, two orange, one red, from the central stem of the leafy plant. And how his mouth would have puckered, the berries, slightly tart.

He walked the rocky soil, maneuvering through sharp rocks. The land filled up until he felt

1: p93 • 1

swallowed by the edges, the browns and greens, rocks and stones, roots and leaves, pieces of shell and bone. Beyond, the melodic, flashing sea. Above, the blanketing sky.

While he communed with the mountain, the berries doing most of the work, the students and

2: p9 • 1

teachers searched for him, calling both names, Menelaus and Tom, into the quiet blue sky. The day went by. Each hour of his absence measured. Each, in his own way, feeling responsible for what, as the sun began to set, felt like his demise.

When he eventually returned, we embraced him and offered him water. He drank the first cup

3: p172 • 3

and with glassy, pinning eyes, said he'd seen us from a ledge as we walked among the rocks. "I was so thirsty and no one would let me drink from his bottle!"

Two days later, we put him on an airplane bound for home. He whispered to me that one day he would write a good story and send it.

Every spring, I pass the leafy plants. Some days, quietly desperate for a little adventure, I contemplate the possibility of picking a berry or two, sour and sliding down my throat. But even the smile-mouthed goats know to stay away from the leafy green *mandragora*. A plant without a friend like Menelaus who, despite his promise, never sent a story.

Poison

Areti's long hair was black, her wrists were tiny. In any weather, she wrapped herself in a beat-up leather jacket. *1: p3 • 1*

She went through the boys like paper napkins, then used up the girls as well. *2: p50 • 3*

Even I, seasoned teacher, drank her poison and found it sweet. *3: p93 • 2*

Gypsies

Circe and Odysseus had spent the previous two hours sitting in church pews listening to Byzantine chants. Easter, two days away.

Outside St. Nicholas Church, a gypsy woman approached them. She held out a dark, handless stump. In the crook of her other arm, she stored something swaddled in sheets.

Odysseus sent the gypsy away with a gesture. "Man, it's so obvious there's no baby."

"Can you lend me a ten?" Circe asked.

Odysseus muttered, "You're crazy," but pulled out a note. Circe placed it in the crook of the gypsy's arm, beneath the head of the bundle.

Another gypsy approached and stood beside her. This one had two good hands and no bundle.

"Hey," Circe said, "I don't have any more money. That was it."

Odysseus watched her pull the black lycra shirt over her head. Beneath it, a lacy peach bra, pale skin. She handed the shirt to the gold-toothed gypsy who held it to her nose then threw it to the ground. Odysseus grabbed Circe's hand. Steered her past the gypsies and into the late-night souvlaki joint. All the candles had gone out in the church of St. Nicholas.

Tear Gas

The students sat on uncomfortable couches, letting themselves be educated. Outside, the hibiscus were in bloom.

"The air," he said, "was thick. We lit fires with anything we could find—it's the only way to neutralize tear gas—then stood beyond the iron gates of the Polytechnic. Tanks rolled up and down Patission St. We handed out mimeographed fliers to the people waiting for the streetcar. In the next two days, innocent students were killed."

Their teacher had sparkling blue eyes, bushy gray hair, and ruddy skin. He broke off speaking and looked away. Their eyes followed his, trying to see tear gas, fires, tanks rolling down an ordinary street.

Helen

Drinking raki from a tiny clear glass, Helen told me she was looking for an Odysseus. She hinted that she'd once had a Jesus. Evidently years before there'd also been a Rasputin. Her last boyfriend, she said, had been a nobody.

I asked: "But who will you be to this guy? Penelope or Circe? Kalypso? Nausikaa? Where do you put yourself in the timeline of this Odysseus' life?"

"I'll fall where I may. Voyage or Homecoming. No Trojan Wars."

In the background, tourists applied suntan lotion. The ice cubes in their Nescafe frappes clinked, releasing watery puddles.

I remember when she first arrived, wearing American jeans and colorful t-shirts.

Eventually, she located the man she called Odysseus. Within weeks, she'd abandoned everything she owned, walked the streets in a toga.

Some boreal wind must have scooped up her clothes, strewn them across the Aegean peninsula. A batiked Grateful Dead t-shirt down by the rock where we swim. A pair of worn jeans stuck on the thorns of an orange rose bush.

SOUND TRAVELS

The evening was clear. From the top of the mountain, she looked down toward the sea. Goats and sheep moved through the valley of sharp aspalathus, tin bells clanging.

She heard the cries, then found their source: the woman's body was tanned, his was pale. They were fucking in a forest of dwarf pines, half-eaten by the goats.

Beyond them, the road and then the sea, all the way to the horizon.

1: p65 • 2

WRITING

The student, who is almost a man—though small for one, with dainty hands—begins to seduce the girl far away in Canada, but only through writing everything down for the woman, his teacher. To her, he can write anything at all.

She picks up his blue notebook, reads it in the quiet of her house. The boy's not put off by the possibility that her husband may be there beside her, may be kissing her while the blue notebook, his blue notebook, labored over, is placed on the kitchen table, while she and the man who is her husband may find themselves dancing toward lovemaking, stepping across the tile floor of their house, knowing exactly what they are about to do.

That thought doesn't bother him as he boils water for tea. Everything—lighting the gas stove, the voices from upstairs asking him to add more water, the spoonful of honey—mixes with thoughts of his notebook and the words he's written for the older woman, or the girl, or possibly the woman's husband.

2: p152 • 1

He thinks he can see the girl in her kitchen, about to peel a tangerine. Rain comes down against the street below her window. Here, too, rain washes the road. When he walks outside, it wets his nearly ecstatic face.

[Balboa & Great Highway]

1: p175 • 3

let's just say I needed a walk around the block
hustling the sand for a stake next to the weeds
a yellow you can't quite rub off the curb tawny
until you spend an hour at an angle

2: p193 • 5

there's the ruins and the way new things ruin every
good old thing you ever came to depend on
when you dimmed the lights and your room crept in
or some time later you learned to sneak out

3

                                    your window's
not only a west facing portal the best sex ever had
was across the street totally impressive how far

4: p181 • 1

misery would carry if the moon's teeth weren't quite so loud
on the water

5: p98 • 5

all roads eventually lead you to roaming
some things are planned mathematically and appear
in flawed arrangement

6: p172 • 2

when maps are straighter than streets

§§§§

…going to have to get a girlfriend off the Internet   *1*
              if I don't find one soon,
because even though
I'm used to not being with someone
              it gets lonely and old after a while
I really feel like I'm not that undesirable
              I think in high school you used to be super attractive
       that's a fucking cool idea,
       like when I had dredlocks and a beard
              like not by the end of high school
              that was the Elvis year
       I don't think I know what you're talking about
              I don't think I do either
now tell me about how attractive I was
              They used to call you the sun god
       no, see I think I'm pretty good looking now
       and some days I think I look better than almost everyone out there.
              I think in high school you just had a certain sexual aura:
              you had a thing going, with the pot and the dredlocks…
I have been able, in my life, to sleep with very attractive women   *2: p39 • 1*
and I don't want that to stop
              that's what I'm saying, in high school
                     that was especially prevalent
I've come to believe that I can score chicks that are extremely good looking
              but only if they have some little other thing
                     and that that's my niche
                            and this is something that happens
                                   like every three years
                     so I've been banking on the fact
                            that I can pull this off again

and that girls who are interesting
in other things other than looks
get fewer and fewer
as you get older

I don't care what a chick has except that she's beautiful,
but I think that being gorgeous adds all these things to a girl.

At a certain level of beauty it's impossible for a girl to be normal
and not to have become interesting precisely because she's beautiful.

[Market & 16th]

Yesterday, while walking home from the Castro, I had a premonition: I am going to run into someone I know.

In the intersection of 16th street and Market I saw V, and V saw me, and I thought Ah, the fulfillment of the prophecy.

V looked happy to see me—her face woke up and she tipped onto the balls of her feet—oh, hello—as if I were her personal discovery. It has been thirty-six days since we broke up; we were together for a year.

She was still tall. She looks like a gangly, broad-shouldered teenager, or a muscular Patti Smith on the *Horses* album, her choppy black hair wagging in her angular face. I had forgotten how, when her hazel eyes, black eyebrows and smooth Irish/Canadian skin all fall together, she's lovely. She can be ugly too, the blunt jaw and sharpness and fear take over. V is like one of those psychology illusion pictures: princess/witch, princess/witch.

How are you? I asked.

Oh, I'm fine, she said. Hey, my sister got a goat. She laughed and fanned her long fingers at each side of her head. It has little goat ears and a little goat mouth. I got to feed it a bottle, just like in the movies, you know, Heidi or something. She laughed again—it made me happy to see V laughing.

1: p45 • 1

Two months ago she would have come back to my apartment and we'd have fucked in our jeans on the couch, these prehistoric sounds coming out of my throat—who knew those sounds were in me? V made me marvel at my own body; I thought anyone who could elicit such primal music would save me from something, the everyday I guess. Once, we talked about adopting kittens and buying a house together, and then my imperceptible unhappiness evolved into gross unhappiness. A week before I started this project, I adopted Spot and Fido on my own.

2: p204 • 3

V lit a cigarette but did not give me her strong glare—only this far away, disappointed look across Market Street as smoke drifted between the gap in her front teeth. I was sorry to see her smoking again, but I said nothing, because it would only make her mad.

3: p222 • 1

In Harvest Market I bought a ginger beer, then I walked to Petpourri and bought Spot and Fido a crocheted ball stuffed with catnip. At home I tied the ball to a piece of white string (the one that was hanging from the track light on the ceiling) and dragged the ball into the kitchen. The kittens chased it. I dragged the ball into the bedroom. I dragged the ball from one end of my home to the other until the string let go and the ball flew off and got lost in all my junk under the bed. Then I propped pillows on my couch, read student papers, and stared out the dirty windows.

4: p201 • 2

The wild, renegade parakeets are squawking in the palm trees on Dolores, and on 15th Street a young man breaks into ballsy gospel at the top of his lungs. He flings his arms into the air.

V is still in love with me, which makes me feel sad, but also happy. And for a moment, while I lie on the couch surrounded by student papers, I feel a bloating. An irresponsible, iridescent shine.

to a prof. of american romanticism on the effects of reading doestoevsky at age 17

my friend sten is a poet—he is writing   1: p204 • 1
new rules
he displays them—
in the vestibule for the weather: one is a
lopsided bird perpetually
ruffling
perpetually sodden feathers.

another is the proud
lumberjack
wearing shiny copper buttons and denim
with rips and runs
in incremental spiral.

the newest rule is a fresh fat
halibut, he hands it to me and i hang it—
from a hook.

sarah's favorite one   2: p27 • 1
is the airplane (guidance, architecture):
hope of post-card writers who dream
awake of sleep
and hissing beaches.

the form for rules is that of logical, optical,
and western
skeletal imperative. a grenade
in the shape of a fishing rod. a big
coat. mount rainier is a skin and every sense of rule
has to hold its innards from
elevation-inspired decompression.   3: p161 • 1

it is thus his
head i admire most—to move through a room or a meal
is to move at incredible speed—chased by wolves
or broken pieces of plate.

lately we instruct
each other
on how to have visions.

visions may be fists or snowy shoulders.
visions may be
history, visions may be

visitors. a visitor may be etched onto the old
hidden wallpaper—

1: p18 · 4

in the scene of a swollen womb or swallowed
by fiercest throat or wind
before any poem or residence that is a poem—

but i forget i am elucidating rules.
my favorite, the bear scuttling
away dancing or galloping
(each mark on the page a bit of clawed mud)

her strong jaws delighting in sten's
severed, congealing, and clearly speaking
head.

§§§§

I've got these great cows in the sky
and lemonade clinking
        as an image.
They would move really slowly,

        can't write a whole poem by recording
problem is that I'll generate these little bits
            disjointed,
what's good is that
you don't just write the next thing,
            you turn it off
                    when you're not inspired
        and then you stop

and the reason why you wouldn't want to do something about it
is precisely because you want it to have the providential character
        of faith
you make something and you just have to think that it will turn up;
        one thing happens, gathers salt,
        "first of all you have to be a great storyteller"
        that's what they say on TV about making movies

        only one man could make a point with his characters
        the only time characters have had serious intellectual things to say
        but they're not just placeholders is in the Brothers Karamazov;
                maybe it's that you need the character to be less smart than you
so Joyce could do it with Stephen Daedelus in *Portrait*
because Stephen sounds childish;
        people don't have very many ideas
and so for someone to have a character
who had more than one idea

1

almost impossible,
maybe you just give them your half-assed proposals.

§§§§

1   With the Mountain Goats songs and the Neutral Milk Hotel repertoire
        I can play a whole hipster folk review.
No, I'm serious. You should hear me.
When haven't you thought that?
No, I'm serious. You should hear me.
That's what you say every time you think you're great.
But now I think I'm actually really good.
I think it's really funny that you don't remember saying that every other time.
        Where you're like, I think I'm actually better than other people.
No, I'm serious.
I know, but that's what you say when you're serious.
I know, but when you realize that you think you must be wrong.

§§§§

2   The other angle
            is
wouldn't it be phat
to be a founding member of a school of poetry?

            but you can't just have a group of friends like that
                    just because it sounds cool
            you have to be born into it
                    by your tip
            and those friends have to exist
                    circumstances have to exist
            and your temperament.

Besides, foundings are

some of the craziest things to go down.

Always violent if you call them that and never by consent.

What about the reunification of Germany?

I don't know if it gets out of the problem,

that's all I'm saying.

§§§§

Been using these pocket folders,   *1*

     using the small yellow notebook

     and then putting the pages into the folder for later typing.

I need to come up with a new system.

I generate a new system every week.

But the multiple systems angle, while fun, doesn't really organize you.

Yeah, I have at least six types of notebook and notecards and the computer.

For me it comes down to well, if I come up with a cool idea I should just remember it

because I'm not going to go through all the notebooks to find it.

I should at least learn how to keep better notes for class.

I actually wish that I understood the purpose of notes for class better.

I keep them, especially from my Nietzsche class, because every day

     the professor was dropping bombs.

And you can't possibly remember them off the top of your head.

One of his students has notes from his class since the '80s   *2: p152 • 10*

and has them all perfect and in binders.

     I'm gonna copy them.

He should publish them.

He's only published one book and by all accounts it's really hard.   *3*

If you can do that and you love teaching, that's amazing.

You have to be pretty ensconced in the department, not now.

If you get ensconced you can get pretty weird.

If you're allowed to get weird, you'll go there, no problem.

Dear Y,

For my parents' wedding, the elderly monsignor, a man who had overseen masses for many decades and knew my mother and her relatives, asked especially to marry them. Then, at the wedding, during the vows, he said: "Do you... Do you... what's your name?" to my mother. She responded tersely with her name. Then he turned to my father and asked, without a pause, "Do you, Buddy Fry, take Jane Funk?" My father slammed down his booklet and said: "I'm James Wagner!" Later on, my mother had to start another section of the mass because the monsignor didn't remember it. And finally, as the ceremony ended, he intoned, "And I forbid the pagan ceremony of throwing rice."

§§§§

when you're in your early 60s, if you're in good health,
        you're pretty much at the top of your game as a philosopher,
    enough experience
        without wear—
            poets are young
        and they seem like they get worse
that's where being ensconced is a real problem
      once you get the knack
      you can just go
    and maybe not saying anything anymore.
Ashbery can make an Ashbery poem whenever he wants,
        constant generation,
    but there's always hope
          you never know what you might be good at
           that you haven't tried yet,
      like I've never been skiing;
            I hope you never ski…
also glad I'm not a taxi driver,
    not knowing how to drive would really make that job suck,
how did I find myself here:
      or the operator of a lock and dam:
      OH SHIT, THE LOCK!

§§§§

      …don't think I want to travel to India.
realized a long time ago,
      anywhere else you want to go?
    Japan

just for style, minimalism,

just a really distinct, well-articulated, aesthetic,

strange morality: I mean where do you get warlords?

In Afghanistan, the shittiest country in the whole world

and then you say, if warlords are a factor

refined and ugly

semi-permeable

yet well articulated…

but obviously Japanese people have an inner life,

but do people have an inner life in North Korea?

Let's pretend like they do, watching reality TV in their heads,

but I really think people can be brainwashed.

§§§§

when you said it didn't matter the type of book you read.

I just think I can just read books well,

I was interpreting the hell out of this Kafka parable,

and I was like

I know this is right:

"point of the myth is to situate the interpreter in time and space

part within a whole;

interpreter as part, unless you will never belong"

whereas, the interpreter of the parable

is completely anonymous,

instead of situating, dislocates;

takes you precisely out of time and place,

forces you on yourself"

and fake myths situate people better than any other

but I think that's money,

money in the bank;

written a lot of poetry as something,

but then always satire,

could poetry actually be something else?

to stand on its own.

like the Ion

I want to write a book called
And Are You The Best General, Ion?
always ideas for books, but don't merely take a weekend,
passages and interpretations
about reading esoteric texts, clumped,
if you don't have an axe to grind it's cooler
and if you're not trying to be a virtuoso,
but they'll be real interpretations of different shit
done soberly
but it would be strange because
you probably didn't think
the book was about that

[Market & McAllister]

Who if scratched would reveal a person
Was leaning against the wall
1: p222 • 4   by a subterranean newsstand
When someone palmed him
2: p92 • 3   A quick lot of money
And flung all available from the open rack
(random, flying headlines covering an infirm retreat).

3: p177 • 2   'It was strange,' said the newsboy,
Who'd walked away for a moment.
'I came back, they were gone.'
The policeman nodded: 'See anyone?'

4: p75 • 1   15 years old and standing off to the side:
one hand balled into a fist,
boil pocks down his legs,
dirty shirt, wild makeup, darting eyes.

[Church & 15th]

Always sitting outside this worn wood-and-lacquer box of a café,
chest chain-mailed in punkish buttons. "SMACK!" his story goes,
taps his ashes like a girl, and catches my anthropological eye very
much off-guard. San Francisco is clod and rainy this time of yard
and my anthropomorphic eyes wander about his shorts and shot
sleeves. He tales his store over and oven, loudening the "SNACK!"
inch team. Ay dismember if singe hum befall, and lever gnome
who to tyke hiss snail.

1: p90 • 1

GROTESQUE

1: p104 • 1

some morning coiled subway in stations,
the way of empty promise. rideau street
makes aware the routes of proximity.

three wrongs make it; pencil-thin and red
dragons awake, the night halloween
forgets, stops being a question.

2

are you getting this? are you backbiting
unrehearsed beauty?

a terrible mode of grotesque.

1: p173 • 2

1   Dear V,

2: p10 • 1   The fog and bus and child.

Do flies buzz? Note the imprecision of all the different types of buzzing. But when we hear one buzzing—through constant usage the particular sound of the buzzing is heard when we mention the fly. It is buzzing pre-buzzing. It's a drag.

3: p175 • 3   I guess I suppose maybe I thought.

4   There is a breeze—well, there are many separate breezes. I am going around town looking for bread, stumbling into a place with metal doors with graffiti on them. There is not bread there, but there is beer and an owner with a sports hat on, a thin cotton T-shirt, and he's bending at the waist, looking for something beneath the counter. We carry on a small conversation. He remains in the same position for the duration, and I eventually leave.

5: p18 • 1   "Some ghosts grow very fat if they get plenty to eat. They are very fond of honey." (Hurston, *Mules and Men*)

[15th & Ramona]

Clifden Moth, earwig, true bug, ant yellow mother, cockroach, house cricket, glowworm, bush cricket, dragonfly, walking stick, squash bug, ground beetle, goat moth, leaf hopper, rove beetle, true bug, tiger moth, ground bug, praying mantis, checkered beetle, honey bee, ladybug, weevil, human flea, horsefly, dragonfly, fire bug, diving beetle, stag beetle, homet, caddis fly, longhorn beetle.

Two Mormon boys wearing backpacks walk toward Guerrero. They look clean, nice. They appear to have no grit or irony. One of them seems, for a moment, to offer a promise of sullenness, a slack in his walk, the hem of his pressed blue pants almost touching the sidewalk, but I think it's just his shoe isn't fitting him right.

1: p218 · 4

[Market & 12th]

1: p100 • 1

My neighbor comes out of his studio cocoon across the hall. We never talk because he is inside himself. He is packed in gel. Sometimes on my walk to work down Market Street I walk behind him and we don't speak but I send him human love and he knows I'm there. Or at least I imagine he knows I'm there. His legs turn out as he walks and he has small hips. He is small all over and he has curly sandy-blonde hair, and he has eyes but I can't see them. The faded tape on his mailbox says his name is Andrew. Once I tried to send him a touch like in the German movie *Wings of Desire* when Peter Falk touched those in despair. I stared at Andrew's back and wove a spell: may Andrew feel loved today, may Andrew not feel alone today. This could be extreme arrogance.

These are my kittens, I say. I introduce him to Spot who has no spots and Fido who looks nothing like a Fido and he bends down and wiggles his fingers.

Hello, he says.   Hello. Kitty. Kitty.

I stare at him. Spot and Fido stare at him. I wish they would climb on Andrew and kiss his face, I wish they would leap into his arms and purr, but they back off and puff and spit. Andrew's fingers begin to look ridiculous in the air so I throw their mouse out into the hall and they forget about dissing Andrew. I start to babble about how I'm trying to increase their territory and Andrew backs off into his apartment like he's trying to get away from me.

SWEET RINGO

Ringo Starr is my neighbor. Nobody except him ever enters or leaves his apartment yet every night I hear loud, Liverpudlian sex. Then crying. All night, every night: sex and crying. He must not know that the walls are paper thin. Sometimes, if he stands before his lamp just so, he is silhouetted on my wall—like an egg in front of a lit candle. Because of this I learned he has a third arm. A small third arm, like that of a T-Rex. I imagine this would be advantageous for a drummer, but in all these years I have never heard him drum. As far as I can tell, he is not sad for the Beatles. I listen. That band is never mentioned. Despite his many tears and passions and ideals, he is a sober man. He lets his phone ring and ring.

Ringo Starr has sex for hours but I wonder with whom. I imagine the third arm is advantageous. *1: p205 • 1* It is not pornography played loudly: the woman screams his name. His real name is Richard Starkey. She screams Ringo! Richard! Dick! She is a filthy woman. He deserves much better. If I turn out my lights I can smell her.

Ringo Starr is a very bad driver. He crashes inexpensive cars almost daily. Probably this is because his mind is always occupied with big ideas and plans for our betterment as a species. One day his car will return to his space with a cracked windshield, the next day a dented bumper, then he'll have an eventful day and return home with the car leaking fluids, hardly steerable, smashed, scratched, and dented all over—until he can drive it no longer. At least once a month there's a new cheap car in his space. His celebrity status must get him out of tickets. Our city has no public transport. I want to offer him a ride, but then he'd be obliged to reciprocate, and I fear riding in his passenger seat.

Ringo Starr moves his bowels only once every nine or ten days—and when he finally does, he apologizes to his turds before flushing them. Such is his empathy, but I worry for his health. Eat more salad, I want to say but don't. Some nights I hear dancing—clomp clomp—but no music. Never music. I think he has become disillusioned about music, its inability to initiate real change, despite all that it promises. As a courtesy, I too refrain from playing music. I have gathered that his chief horror is that he wants to be neither buried nor cremated. I would suggest a sea burial to him, but I'm afraid it would solve his indecision, and then he might allow himself to die, and then whose fault would it be but mine?

I have gathered more: Ringo Starr wants the Constitution changed so he can run for President. *2: p184 • 1* He will make healthy food taste good and unhealthy food taste bad. He will make all rivers reverse direction so the oceans will empty themselves onto the land and the seabed will be exposed so mankind may live on it and thus the world will seem new. Then he will outlaw dishonesty.

He will invite the moon to come closer. Every night I hear him speak of these plans yet he never begins trying to enact them. Instead it's sex and tears. Every night I tell myself, Tomorrow I will knock on his door. Tomorrow I will offer my assistance. Tomorrow things will begin to change and never stop changing. Ringo, I will say, sweet Ringo, tell me how I can help.

24

…my mind obsesses, knowing no one innocent. Wherever I look, out of the sultry, yearning waves, 24 like a Venus rises. Let my adoration become a hymn. In her, the sensual source of all my desiring. My hormones have set sail toward a long sought treasure crying: "Thar she blows!" My senses are on fire. I can't ignore her. I first encountered her, covered in ink, flirting with fractions on a page. God, I swear she had nothing on underneath!

1: p199 • 1

Through my numbered wilderness I wander, dreaming of the sensual abstraction I want above all else, questioning my salty, passionate yearning. At my back, fertile stands of cedar, myrtle, fir and oak, ancient groves of primal numbers, pagan in their intensity. Homer would have known this place. And Pythagoras. Who can say what Paris thought as he breathed in the color of Helen's terrible, lovely eyes and in that dreaming touched the profound center of his own destruction; the death of all things rational. A cellular fire burns up the sacred seconds of our experience, like a sculptor it begins with too much clay. In the wash of my secret fantasies, I wallow.

Why are we made so strongly physical but to celebrate the sexual in ourselves? In my tortured forest, each fertile thought becomes a number. Each imagined number, a vessel with which to multiply. When numbers speak, my earth shakes and I'm thrown into an emotional pitch where the miraculous explodes as I exhale. I dreamed of God's face. He came to me in the shape of a number. In the garden of our souls a cold corruption grows. It is the lost child's animal cry of surrender as we move deeper into the truth of ourselves, realizing our strength is no strength, but a force of movement keeping us afloat as we swim, dance and flail:

Moving from moment to moment,
we are what we must be.
Deep in our own imperfection we come
at last
to realize,
ours is a will too fragile for eternity.

2: p143 • 3

Oh, but to share these thoughts with 24, naked in my bed!

3: p180 • 1

13   PUB. BY L. STERN, BROOKLYN, N. Y.   Arverne Hotel, Arverne-by-the-Sea.

1: p99 • 2

WHEN MY FAMILY OWNED ARVERNE'S
BIGGEST HOTEL, MY FAVORITE
PLACE TO PLAY WAS AT THE TOP
OF THE LEFT-HAND TURRET,
THE ONE CLOSEST TO THE
OCEAN, HERE I COULD BE LEFT
ALONE BY DAY TO LOOK AT THE OCEAN
AND THE BATHERS, SOMETIMES WITH MY
TELESCOPE. IN THIS LITTLE ROOM, I
HAD MY EARLIEST EXPLORATORY SEXUAL
EXPERIENCES,   *Richard Kostelanetz*

FOR ROBERT BLAKE'S SAKE

"It's always been the same thing—the old have to be killed by the young."

—*Robert Blake,* In Cold Blood

"It's always been the same thing—the young have to be killed by the old."

—*Robert Blake,* Lost Highway

I was the youngest, and my father, Robert Blake the first, made it a practice to never directly address me—using either my mother when she was out on bail or asking my sister when the situation became too urgent for someone not to speak. He would say things like, "Lenore, could you tell Robert to 'shut the hell up' and to 'never do what he just did in my presence again?' " All the while he'd be mussing up my hair with his hand like he was putting out a cigarette with his shoe: "Huh, Lenore, hon, could you tell him if he does that again I'll 'remove his kidney while he's sleeping' and 'sell it for lunch money next week?' Could you dear, because I would myself, but you can see what I'm doing here, can't you?"

He always said it was silly and a little absurd to talk to me like that, but then again, so was the experience of bringing a child into the world and trying to tell it what and what not to do.

At dinner parties, during the six months of my life that I was certifiably cute, he would farm out anecdotes and punch lines to me by passing notes to the women he found attractive or flagging down servants carrying martinis. He gave me a walkie-talkie when I was 7 and made people talk to me only through that until I was almost 12. Sometimes it would just be him hiding in a different room and disguising his voice when he couldn't find anyone else to do it for him.

A few hours before he died when I was in college he wrote a note to me on a paper airplane and paid a male nurse $50 to deliver it by hand to my dorm room at 3 a.m.:

> "Come quick. Stop. Terribly urgent. Stop. Reports of my recovery overblown
> and optimistic. Stop. Let me gird my loins with the sight of your face one last
> time. Stop. No, really."

When I showed up, he tried to act like he didn't see me standing in the doorway on the other side of the room. He tried to act like I was catching him right in the middle of something, something that, if I were quiet and kept my head down long enough, I would be able to spy on it too, seeing a secret pocket of the same secret thing: like a ritual or underground initiation, Black Mass or the Masons—my persistent Pappy Blake promising me that, for behaving, he'd show me something no one else had ever seen, something of which Lenore or mom wouldn't even know what to think:

He kept leaning over the side of his bed, like he'd dropped his bedpan out the window or something, with his back to me for the longest time. It looked broken, like chipped teeth biting crookedly down on his spine while the rest of his body scrambled, all of him trying to pull something I couldn't see up into bed with him. And it occurred to me that I had never seen my father without his shirt. Not without smoking jacket and pipe or sleeveless cotton top before bed. Never not-wearing the heavy burlap shop apron mixed with sawdust or yard-work denim. He was like the father mannequin in the Sears window—changing for days of the week and seasons but little else, a kind of clotheshorse trying on roles for me, business casual, Robert, or maybe you prefer evening wear: "Tell him he would, Lenore, say, 'You would prefer evening wear, Robert, wouldn't you?' Say it now, now and just like that."

His shoulder blades scraped against each other as he started to turn—shovel heads hanging too close in his shed—and his body kept clenching, pitted and stretched thin, going translucent in places. I didn't know if disease could do that to him, collapse him from the inside, layer after layer run through and spit out its mouth. But in a perverse way, his sickly moving body reminded me of Lenore, the private language she and I had when we were kids, able to tell each other that things would be okay with our hands, sign language or tapping Robert Blake code in discrete places on our bodies when he was around and wouldn't allow us to otherwise speak.

1: p196 • 1

And then, still bent over and not facing me like he was, I heard him say something; I realized, with nobody else in the room, he must be finally talking directly to me. He popped back up onto the bed quick, all of a sudden, like an animal—like that—and I didn't sit down because I saw what he was holding:

He had a dirty gun-sack with my grandfather's gun in it, the over-under looking just like it did the summer I found it wrapped in newspaper in their bedroom closet. His two-ply, double-insulated orange hunting jacket was draped over the window sill where he'd shed it, but he was still wearing its accompanying duck-ear hunting cap. Like usual, he'd stretched and tied the hat's flaps in such a way so they either covered or cast in a shadow his entire face: since we were kids it had been his practice to regularly, through screens and subtle touches—long scarves or concealer spots—keep his face a secret. It was the way he liked to treat us: drawing our attention to what was wrong only to forbid us on its face—to make sure that we knew that he knew, that there was a question and something was off but we couldn't ever expect to ask what:

2: p170 • 3

He held the gun with two hands, palms up, arms out like I was a king and it was my scepter—like he was knighting me with what was left of his body, giving me my birthright or something even though he would've never done that in real life. And he had this mock humility he'd never shown me either, looking down, an embarrassed third-grader on stage for the Christmas play or Springtime Jubilee, except he was in bed, so he was staring at his stomach, maybe wondering why it looked so strangely inflated, pot-bellied like a starving Ethiopian's even though he was solidly mid-American.

3: p166 • 2

He was still talking, like we'd been interrupted in the middle of a conversation, like we'd been having the same one our whole lives, passing notes back and forth in class that turned out to be our long names when we were done:

"…and you know I always took what your ex-mother gave me and made what I could. You know I was the only thing that kept you kids boxed up and ready to move like a good father should.

"And I may never have said it, but that was because I knew you were never really listening… you little dunderhead—"

I had to grab the gun that he'd held up with his arms the whole time because he was going purple now and not so steady, and I was afraid it might go off if he dropped it. Except I realized all of sudden that everything was happening in reverse, not like I thought at all. Because when I took the gun, it dropped him; like he was a coat hanging off a hook unscrewed unexpectedly from the wall. He wasn't giving me the gun because I had had it the whole time:

1: p175 • 1

"Tell Robert he's got it all wrong, and I'm sick of holding my tongue just so I don't hurt his feelings."

His body started balling up in places where it shouldn't have been able to, a sinkhole swallowing itself, dollar bills crumpling up in somebody's fist after sidewalk bait and switch. And as I felt myself starting to shrink—somehow suddenly too short to see him over the chart hanging at the end of his bed—all I could think was: "Well, look at what you finally went and did."

2: p172 • 4

§§§§

1   …and being a philosophy professor is unattractive
unless you have joie de vivre, unless you
also lead a poetic life
you are a miserable miserable man
                    waiting for something that may never happen
            not some weird bottled up thing, I just don't talk about it,
        as if you throw a stone and don't know what you're doing
                            tragedy of the moral life
                    setting habits in place that are almost impossible to break,
2   sucking a stone for lost water;
        not even sacrificing it for being a philosopher,
                    but for being a reader of philosophy
            and you have to know how much you love that
            and you must have the utmost confidence
                you must bring it and be an arrogant bastard
                    but is that enough to sacrifice the other pleasures of life?

§§§§

do the desires of the elitist have a hearing?
is it accepted? is it tolerated?
are conservatives like me tolerated?
        well, you are here
but you're different from polite society
you've known me for a long time
you have to put up with me…

§§§§

...whether becoming *is*
or whether it's just passing away
            to another world beyond it;
how is that not a problem?
            you're saying
everything is historically conditioned
            except
the fact that everything is historically conditioned;

        otherwise, you have to say
                people will think that for a while, even a long while,
                        and that afterwards people will think something else
            so, nothing,
                    unless you have a vantage point from the end of history,
                            because we do, groundless
doesn't the fact that you believe something for no reason trouble you?
do you not think about your life? do you not take it seriously?
        how do you both think about your life and not think about it?
        how do you as a thinking person discard any notion of value, untroubled?
                you just do what the culture tells you?

§§§§

no, most people aren't relativists,
but most people would like to think of themselves that way;
        that's where the money is
people really want to be tolerant,
            but that's so obviously not true...

precisely the most *cultural* cultures
are the least relativist…

but I won't give you a half-baked argument
about how tolerance has to be tolerant of intolerant.

as if I fight against relativism
because it is the strongest strategy of people who want
everyone to be a pawn in the game:
   easier to manipulate
if they don't believe in anything…
our daily experience sounds silly,
but that's not a refutation;
it seems like a silly refutation
because a 15-year-old could think of it,
but why doesn't it seem like a silly idea
because a 15-year-old could refute it?
   so logically unsound and yet so powerful
 torn
and wish they could think it
but know they can't
   and it may be that political ideas
   must be philosophically half-baked
and you just have to make things work by trial and error,
but people like to argue from principles;
   which way is it better to be wrong?

1: p173 • 1

§§§§

2

Accepting what culture you're given,
   to some extent, but moving beyond it,
   to say *culture is binding and brainwashing*
    makes you sloppy and lazy and watch too much TV.

I choose things that don't make me happy, constantly,

and part of it is my fault
but part of it is that I live where these things are really accessible,
and sometimes I wished I lived in a place that
made its first and only purpose to keep me straight and focused,
and for those reasons I have serious doubts about democracy and liberalism.

I just hate loving things
I'm supposed to love:
You're feeling what's happening now.
This is the world's expression...
A soul is big enough for the high and the low
Except for the fact that we die.

1: p7 • 2

§§§§

How many great books have there been?
More than none.
They've always been possible.
Not before they existed.
Philosophers exist into the future.
Civilized man could fade away.
If there's nothing greater than the perfect fry that we're after
It's the perfect fry, perfect shape, width, etc.
And you're telling me that's not petty?
Why is that petty?
Why is it not? I think the onus is pretty much on you.
It's perfect; it's not the fry that matters, but the perfection
Then why shouldn't we make the goal of America to produce the perfect pair of tits?
I mean the perfect killing gun.
So what about the great man? We don't want everything to be great.
We want them to run the country, to teach us.
Then why should there be any constraints on their power?
The great man wouldn't allow for the perfect French fry.

2

appendix

abeyance: between breast and, *33*

abiogenesis: *vis-à-vis* a son appearing between those legs, *23*

abominations: the grim padres of, *180*

absence: before the mirror confirmed its, *23*; each hour measured, *200*; of singularity, *112*

accuracy: on toast spears for pastlife, *87*

ack-ack: *152*

aftermath: cry of the burn victim in the, *160*

afterthought: strikes distant listeners as an, *160*

agri-alchemy-melancholia: experiments in, *180*

air booty: *68*

alcohol: panicky memories filled with, *143*

all-nighter: from what forms the whispering in your kitchen cupboards, *168*

America: *vis-à-vis* institutions sustaining themselves, *141*; *vis-à-vis* the perfect pair of tits, *235*

ammo: *152*

animals: *vis-à-vis* shoot vs. sell, *82*

ankle: in my grip, from under the bedsheet, *12*

answer: rum and Coke, *137*

answer desk: *vis-à-vis* acne burning, *81*

appetite: for this appetite, *61*

apple: fit me like the skin of an, *39*; red, with a broken neck, *101*; apples: mad, out of nowhere, *105*; mug, mask, ash, *195*; When the law comes I will tell them we are, *100*

apprenticeship: of forgetting, *199*

aquarium: impenetrable, *58*

archer: associated with the arrow, *193*

arizona: I hated you most in, *58*

arm: Ringo Starr's third, like that of a T-Rex, *225*

arrow: associated with the archer, *193*

ash: mask, marbled, apples, *195*

ass: Why did I drink so much and act like an, *143*

assassination: of the notion of reality, *178*

background: *vis-à-vis* an etching that resembles a water ode, *168*; opacity haunts in the, *169*

bag: chance is a, *76*; *vis-à-vis* powder, slipped over the top of the glass, *19*; soaking in the dark, *110*

banishment: the threat of, *144*

bank: fucking money in the, *144*

Barbie: another fookced up, *73*

bartender: I will say to the doctor, *100*

basin: a self-created cistern of dark, *7*; the melody of the connection when they kissed, *73*; basins: fill to the brim with the brackish runoff, *164*

beacon: Wal-Mart, whirling to the lost, *89*

beam: into his skull, *150*

beauty: as loss of individuality, *113*; at a certain level, impossible for a girl to be normal, *206*; easier to see because of photographs, *198*; unrehearsed, *220*

bed: legs, that thunka thunka thunka of, *159*; thinking our time passed so quickkly, *58*; with 24, naked in my, *227*; beds: mad photographs and beauty, *198*

bedroom: the glass filled with bees, *19*; walking into the, *13*; where they always return, *16*

bedsheet: *12*

bees: the throat was crammed with, *20*

beginnings: What—happens—here—between—these, *102*

belief: heretofore milk signified, *32*

belt: *vis-à-vis* hearing the echo, *99*

bench: cigarette scarred, *42*

bennies: years of cocaine and, *56*

berries: doing most of the work, *200*

bird: into the rafters, *166*; lopsided, *209*; pushed open into migrant snow, *94*; birds: interred in south-shipped fruit, *195*; open beaked on water, *66*; terrible as a flock of, *61*

birdsex: a window on, *110*

birth: inversion of, *35*

birthday: in that red dress smiling like it was her, *59*; my twenty-fourth, *198*

bitch: according her whip, *4*; by his side, *70*

bivalves: as food, as aphrodisiacs, *23*

black fosse: *vis-à-vis* the dead of his own night, *26*

black line: the water would write, *189*

blade: hacking apart a radio tower, *168*; blades: between his stepfather's lips, *20*; shoulder, pushed together, body contorting, *112*

blind: highway impatient and, *93*; man, *44*; blinds: drawn, in those dingy rooms, *98*; your words were like, *165*

bliss: and blister, *64*

blister: and bliss, *64*

blistering: of his skin, he could hear the, *112*

blood: bits of skin raised to meet the, *4*; flowing to the mask, *161*; in dilution over the curb's lip, *1*; in glittering splendor, *162*; left on the ceiling, *72*; on my pillow, *9*; scribe's already in my, *6*

body: acquired by cheating, *31*; already given over, *94*; aquatic, *164*; as a sink hole swallowing itself, *231*; behind them on a funeral bier, *17*; beneath the cloak, thin, *1*; *vis-à-vis* feeling the creature stir, *112*; genuflected as if disposed at prayer, *18*; innervated by a strangling pleasure, *28*; subdued, ratio of the falling, *72*; tanned, fucking in a forest of dwarf pines, *203*; twin brothers molding their mother's, *35*; Why should I love this, *165*; bodies: covered in wounds, *17*; of strangers, straining to witness the gurney, *2*; parched for liquid, *35*; softening until the membranous parts have dissolved, *164*; tapping Robert Blake code in discrete places on our, *230*

boil pocks: *218*

bombs: Nietzsche professor dropping, *213*

bone: *vis-à-vis* glittering splendor, *162*; in transit, *3*

boobs: touched for like an hour, *39*

book: And Are You The Best General, Ion?, *217*; *vis-à-vis* Missoulian obit, *93*; no Jack Bommb in the, *91*; to end, I know now how I want the, *43*; wildflower, *200*; books: abandoned like old clothes, *152*

border: of skin, *26*

borrowings: scenery, keeps a finch & slows, *191*

bouquet: of relict, *68*

bowels: *vis-à-vis* Ringo Starr moving them, *225*

box: better on top of, *99*; chain-gang, finger tuck voice, *165*; snuff, of self, *158*; to live in a, *151*

Boy Scout awards: *19*

boy toy: *50*

breakdown: my father had a, *51*; self-emulation to the point of, *197*

breast: whatever else was a ~ for but to obey, *33*; breasts: & the long border of skin, *26*; hot and dry under lotion-slick fingers, *21*; never suckled, *35*

bro: *75*

brothers: moistening the materials, *35*

bruise: above the pisiform, *8*

brutality: ordinary, *49*

bruthas: *74*

building: clown particulars, *191*; how many rings does it take to topple a, *188*; lifting rocks and slangin math, *72*

bullshit: *188, 194*

burden: each one was to all those around him, *150*

bus: fog and child, *222*; rides and suicide, *69*

buttocks: inutile, of space-time, *192*

buzzards: waiting in head, *6*

bwai pimp: *71*

bygones: going by, *183*

cage: or mango tree sunlight, *110*

californium: quest for purer, *180*

camera: *23*; But what has the ~ tracked?, *4*; recording the damage, *190*; that could make people real, *6*; this garden ~ & smoke, *191*

Canada: to seduce the girl far away in, *203*

carousel: private, *vis-à-vis* the emblem of passion, *4*

carpet thread: sewn in blood-tipped cross-stitch, *18*

castle: the rambling splendor of Sleaze, *37*

cause: depression is the lake that fills it, *30*

cave: entrance: *172*; not a real one, *178*; caves: sexes dank as, *164*

ceiling: blood left on the, *72*; till it blacks me out with spin, *98*

cells: in a parked SUV, *180*; photoreceptive, *23*

celluloid screen: *vis-à-vis* this mental interlude, *22*

certainty: narrator's logical, that a hand was there, *162*; of the sphere beneath, *112*

chain-gang: finger tuck voice box, *165*

chalk: corpse, hopscotch, *195*; *vis-à-vis* rolling through the window or still, *156*

change: loose, cigarette scarred park bench, *42*; changes: as if my ears were the, *5*

character: giving them your half-assed proposals, *211*

charms: the disjunctive text has its, *169*

chemicals: *vis-à-vis* sniffing, cleaning restrooms, *99*

chessboard: *172, 198*

chest: dead, I pushed my dead hands against your, *165*; stepfather's bare, *20*

chicks: cool, will arise, *140*; extremely good looking, I can score, *205*

childhood: chamfered, flutter of a, *192*

children: *vis-à-vis* playing in the sand, *52*; round, seal them in his house, *14*; should not be confused with the, *166*

Christ: in Wood with Traces, *167*

church: *28, 99*; *vis-à-vis* father yelling in middle of sermon, *52*; made out of what looks like nothing when sober, *27*

cigarettes, 4 punks, *68*; methol, *67*

cipher: cut for wolves, *192*

circumstance: *vis-à-vis* the phat thing, *143*; circumstances: strange, we should begin having sex, *55*; to meet someone (conjecture) under certain, *53*

cistern: of dark, self-created, *7*

citizen: Am I foockin, *72*

city: as relationship, *186*; improvisational, *191*

Cleveland: *60*

closet: broom, wet all week imagining me and Hush, *40*; skin-laden, *87*

cloth: blue twilled, called corpse, *195*; grasp for, yet find only flesh, *163*

cloud: landowner forgetting music inside, *191*; clouds: as sperm whales, *23*; rising in the south, *193*

coat: big, *209*; from the Hasbeen thrift store, *38*; hanging off a hook, like he was a, *231*

code: convinced that I had cracked the, *197*; in discrete places on our bodies, tapping Robert Blake, *230*

{.....}____,_____.(...)+{.....}___!(...): *196*

collar: bridal, his white moustache pressed against her, *52*

collections: I hope to keep discretely, *64*

collision: Exhibit K, *171, 178*; of bad luck and good timing, *154*

comedies: revealed within the hand of the poet, *146*

commentary: twinned sigh across the airshaft, *64*

commitments: to be made all the same, *160*

company: grow old in their mother's, *35*

compositions: of collapse and destruction, *113*

concrete: cyclone wire, part of his leg under the, *110*; split like marble, *198*; upon a living being, piling, *182*

condom: I stole from the men's bathroom, *38*

confessional: darkened, *28*; rights, *37*

configuration: the board's, *169*; configurations: page 24, arranged in various, *152*

connection: when they kissed, *73*

consanguineous: masking the, *161*

consciousness: descried, states of, *90*

constellation: from apology fields, *191*

constitution: water's, *88*

construction: in jars, *175*

contempt: bright, morning, *113*

contexts: *vis-à-vis* enjambment with neighboring information, *174*

contours: of her sex, *35*

convent: hijack liberties of that, *199*

convulsionaries: of saint medard, *17*

cookies: my name began with, *38*; shortbreads robed in Belgium chocolate, *177*

cop: tripping his partner out, *99*

copula: splendid, between film and desire, *22*

corner: a wife in the, *12*; of somerset harbours holes in the ground, *156*; when some from a, *111*

corpse: hopscotch chalk, *195*; the writer associated with the, *193*; corpses: perfect little, encrypted, *194*

corset-stays: bone, *163*

cotter pin: kicked off the ledge: *172*; was genius, *178*

courthouse: got married at a, *52*; roof, gunners on a, *195*

crackers: scrappin over the betty, *70*

craft: & blow up the knows of the, *68*

craftwork: as strategic self-defense, *194*

creature: *vis-à-vis* the building hunger, *112*

Crest: as prose poem, *153*

crime: against reality, arraigned for, *177*; against reality, being convicted of: *170*

cripples: pooling, *68*

criz: *69*

cross-stitch: blood-tipped, along the lips, *18*

crown: hive for lavender, *191*

cucumber: English, *vis-à-vis* his johnnie, *39*; English, *vis-à-vis* skin-laden closet, *87*

culture: the unknowing, uncaring mercy, *150*

cup: *vis-à-vis* glassy, pinning eyes, *200*; infernal, of debauchery, *22*; when thirsty, the weight of, *154*

curtains: shower, when the princess bathed, *37*

dark: disappearing behind the trees, *44*; I am yours only in the, *165*; screams, rousing mules, *90*; shapeless, over there in the, *47*; soaking a blue bag in the, *110*

darkness: beyond, *112*; how easily we're passing through all this, *59*; radiant, the experiment posterity makes of, *180*

dark side: side, she's on the, *75, 110*

daughter: watercolor, *53*; *vis-à-vis* "Who are you," *52*

daylight: when we most need it, *114*

dead: a question of what's, *16*; eyes of the, *163, 176*; letters, secondary duplication, *154*; mama, *vis-à-vis* ain't watchin me right now, *98*

debauchery: the infernal cup of, *22*

decision: not to look over the frozen water, *94*

definitions: funny, pleasure had some, *149*

democracy: and liberalism, serious doubts about, *235*; couldn't vote for, *165*

demonstrance: the do unto others, *87*

depressive: *vis-à-vis* gesticulations toward order, *49*

desire: film and, the splendid copula between, *22*; prior, a tongue of, *112*; shifting, wedge between the clock & the hrs, *118*; to be in a trance state, *150*; *vis-à-vis* wolves' vacuous mouths, *192*

destroyer: *vis-à-vis* the writing hand, *159*

detective: private, stony leer, *168*

dirt: dirge driven into the, *17*; remains shifting under, *35*; the day's, out from under my nails, *98*

disaster, 80s pop-up, *88*

disease: *vis-à-vis* collapsing from the inside, *230*

disguises: a joke that pokes under a layering of, *65*

disorder: *vis-à-vis* ripped stockings, *178*; sluttish, *22*; history or affective, *108*

divinity: *vis-à-vis* hens rolling in the dust, *193*

dog: black, once i had this, *79*; mangy, eating own vomit, *28*; notion, of a spotting scope's dutiful mistress, *168*; the owner's, King, *41*

dose: time to up my, *61*

doves: carrier, painted, *195*; stapled onto redblue sweaters, *100*

drawer: *vis-à-vis* her bags, *75*; *vis-à-vis* underwear, medals, Boy Scout awards, *19*

dream: *vis-à-vis* fingering her necklace, *165*; installation from a, *65*; of their mother dreaming of them, *35*; *vis-à-vis* seeing his mother again, *25*

dredlocks: sexual aura, with the pot and the, *205*

dresses: *vis-à-vis* a felled-tree's leaves, *198*

duplication: *vis-à-vis* dead letters, *154*; twinning, *50*

dust: blue is a layer of, *175*; hens rolling in the, *193*

dwarf pines: fucking in a forest of, *203*

eagle: stuffed on the QT, *40*

ear: *vis-à-vis* the groove of a man's belt, *99*; ears: as if they were the changes, *5*; cut off, *165*

echo: *75, 110*; from the undisputed king of men, *87*; one cop knew about the, *99*

economy: libidinal, *22*; economies: weak, *vis-à-vis* the disjunctive text, *169*

ecstasy: and anguish, *162*; of saints, *16*

eggs: sucking through pinpricks, *23*

empathy: time for less, *61*

enclosure: day, brachiating into their, *81*

End Man: my very own, *177*

engagement: sportive, something feral in the conditions of, *154*

epilepsy: the waltz leader's, *168*
epiphany: proof vests, *68*
escape: *vis-à-vis* inhaling, *113*
essence: the sword, *199*
excess: stripping off your skin, *162*
excuse: for the tension of a possible storm, *27*
Exhibit K: *171, 178*
experiment: drone of, *154*; that posterity makes of radiant darkness, *180*
eye: a son who is all, *23*; *vis-à-vis* consent, *87*; lidless, lay your pence upon mine staring, *89*; teeth, the loosening of, *62*; whisper hairlash in your, *98*; eyes: blood-blind, *161*; button, of the dead, *163*; in claustrophobic rooms, *195*; little boy in their, *98*; of the dead, *176*; pinning, glassy, *200*; *vis-à-vis* rapture, *177*; serve a movement, *8*; *vis-à-vis* shutting them with dull wire, *165*; singing through the holes of, 165; *vis-à-vis* the damned, *167*; uncertainty in their, 9
eye crumb: *86*
eyelid: epistemic, *192*
face: sister's, on the flute, *45*; while she removed her, *56*; faces: in an old yearbook, *194*; *vis-à-vis* spitting on the law, *100*
failure: *vis-à-vis* Dr. Slatoris, *178*; managed resistance to, *154*; sensory, champagne-like, *161*
father: on the answering machine, *57*; passing away, *51*; *vis-à-vis* the phone, *53*; without his shirt, *230*
faucet: how it evolved, *16*; *vis-à-vis* latex gloves, *19*; to hide from the law, *100*
fencepost: *21*
field: of fetid roses, sexes blooming, *164*; of vision, her legs brace his, *23*; sown with sweat, *195*
fields: apology, exacted backward, *191*
figure: from a Francis Bacon painting, *162*; single, moving, a group of figures is also a, *167*
fill-ins: between relationships, uses her friends as, *50*
film: and desire, the splendid copula between, *22*; remembered, marks lifting a window, *191*; sequential, broken up pieces, *174*
fingers: blank, *14*; lotion-slick, his mother's breasts were hot and dry under his, *21*; *vis-à-vis* inhaling escape, *113*; make things happen, *117*
fish: dead, in his head, *110*
flesh: dull and bloodless, *20*; growing, like a forest, *26*; prophylactic as, *180*; rub the viscosity into your, *161*
flesh-node: attendent, (me), *194*
flirtation: substances not occurring in nature, *180*
flood: the coming, *189*
floor: cellar, damp spots on his, *178*; *vis-à-vis* drugs dropped onto, *59*
fluid: from sexes dank as caves, *164*
Fold: The, *44*

food: aphrodisiacs the mother knows, *23*; bank, lil wigga at the, *71*; buried, so I wouldn't be afraid of starving, *92*
fools: three, ali-ing, *68*
foot: *vis-à-vis* another man's meditations, *113*; clawed, *110*; Grace Kelly's in *Rear Window*, *140*; feet: cut off my, *165*; *vis-à-vis* her mark, *15*; naked, feeling the ground with, *112*; of buzzards waiting in head, *6*; of the hopers, plaster casts, *67*
forest: flesh grows like a, *26*; of clashing erotics, *24*; of dwarf pines, fucking in a, *203*; *vis-à-vis* replacing the house, confusing with children, *166*
forgetting: an apprenticeship of, *199*
foundling: both she-wolf and, *35*
Francis Bacon: *162*
free will: *143*
friend: another, to steal the words of, *162*; clever, everybody needs a, *137*; false, the next person is a, *65*; neighbor, arrested, *85*
fruit: comparing the swelling to, *97*; south-shipped, birds interred in, *195*
fry: perfect, French, *235*
fuck: *vis-à-vis* need, *40*
funeral bier: *17*
game: as a philosopher, at the top of your, *215*; *vis-à-vis* faces rising up afresh, perfect little corpses, *194*; pawn in the, *234*; piece, *169*; poker, winning Pat Walleck's leg, *67*; self-con, *22*
garden: *14*; camera & smoke, *191*; secret, *157*
geodes: *vis-à-vis* sex, *39*
GermX: as prose poem, *153*
gesticulations: toward order, the depressive's, *49*
gesture: his mother's, *25*; repetitive, ugh, what a, *43*; gestures: displaced, *174*
ghost: *111, 166*
gibbet: hang me from the, *165*
girl: *vis-à-vis* beauty, impossible to be normal, *206*; with a scythe, *54*
girlfriend: *vis-à-vis* being shoved down the stairs, *67*; off the Internet, *205*
glass: image of, outside the stream of thought, *53*; *vis-à-vis* shaking until the bees were maddened, *19*; shattered, and toppling, *193*; tiny, drinking raki from a, *202*
gloves: on his stepfather's bare chest, *20*; why do you mock my, *138*
gods: *vis-à-vis* slipping up, *81*
greenery: *vis-à-vis* suburban pointillism, *45*
groceries: *vis-à-vis* Dr. Slatoris, *177*
grotesque: a terrible mode of, *220*
group: of aspirants, unschooled, *160*; of figures, *167*
gun: killing, perfect, *235*
gunnels: of the brood-blown punchers, *86*
gunners: on a Courthouse roof, *195*

gunpowder: art work, *73*

gutter: glittering splendor in the, *162*

habit: prisonhouse of, *154*

halibut: *209*

halloween: forgets, stops being a question, *220*

hallucinogen mandragora: *200*

hand: carving a sliver-moon into my, *192*; glass in my, woke up with blood on my pillow and, *9*; have no, I am so and so and, *162*; sleights of, evermore, *169*; *vis-à-vis* the narrator's logical certainty, *162*; to his throat, *26*; what makes the comedies comedic, *146*; writing, crazed as a hanging judge's, *159*; hands: *vis-à-vis* cutting off and voting for democracy, *165*; dead, against your dead chest, *165*; human, torn down by, *187*; mother's, pulling him in, *21*; over unfamiliar curves, *35*; *vis-à-vis* parting the women's thighs, *164*; plaster casts of, *67*; *vis-à-vis* Robert Blake sign language, *230*; slippery in latex gloves, *19*; soaped, would show you I am ready to cut, *15*; *vis-à-vis* telling her it weren't her fault, *98*; useless appendages, *119*; when you had two, *44*

head: dead fish in his, *110*; feet of buzzards waiting in, *6*; his voice quiet and murmuring in my, *152*; mother's, bent between her legs, *35*; mother's, hidden beneath a floppy straw hat, *18*; *vis-à-vis* moving through a room or a meal, *210*; severed, speaking, *210*; the longest journey, *165*

helix: double, of shame and a terrifying hunger for pleasure, *22*

Hen canyon: *39*

high school: married a guy she dated back in, *52*; *vis-à-vis* the Elvis year, *205*

highway: *vis-à-vis* climbing hills into state forest shadow, *93*; the last stop on his, *98*

hill: wellers, soaking a blue bag in the dark, *110*; hills: black throat of, *94*; climbing, state forest shadow, *93*

hint: of I, *195*

hips: breaching her, in an inversion of birth, *35*; Peter held my, *41*

hit: wanted the, *61*

home: *vis-à-vis* legal notices, *142*; one-time, toward the doorway of his, *161*; something bigger was coming, *27*; song is our only, *195*

honey: spoonful of, *203*; *vis-à-vis* wanting the hit, *61*

hoods: in the offshoot of the alley, *9*

hootie: *39*

hopers: *vis-à-vis* braces, trusses, videotaped mastectomies, *67*

hopscotch: chalk corpse, *195*

horror: *vis-à-vis* Ringo Starr wanting to be neither buried nor cremated, *225*

hot mustard salad: *5*

hotel: *99, 198, 228*

hour: of his absence measured, *200*; hours: alone, vestigial sense of being incomplete in the, *65*; before he died, *229*

house: at times foreign territory she once shared, *152*; his, has made her children round enough to seal them in, *14*; *vis-à-vis* mother getting a job, father having a breakdown, *51*; my last look around the, *189*; on the way to her, *56*; *vis-à-vis* reading the blue notebook, *203*; sometimes a forest replaces the, *166*; *vis-à-vis* thinking of it as age, *111*; *vis-à-vis* two people not giving a shit about anything, *142*; houses: halfway, that crumble, *87*

house-cleaning: psychic, *194*

hunger: building, could taste the, *112*; terrifying, for pleasure, *22*

husband: *203*

hysterectomy: make-nice, *88*

iconography: grim, *82*

id: vs. postmodern gestalt, *158*

idea: in her head that was in my head, *57*; of craftwork as strategic self-defense, *194*

imperative: skeletal, western, *209*

incarnation: sky being part of a promise, *112*; incarnations: funny, pleasure had some, *149*

inertia: comes in silence, *110*; transferred, that once failed Zen, *90*

injections: or a pill would serve, *91*

installation: from a dream, partly observed, *65*

institution: went to see my father at the, *52*

interlocutor: my own self's, *177*

interlude: mental, the imaginary register, *22*

interpretations: of different shit done soberly, *217*

Jean Nate: all prettied up in, *98*

jeune homme: sweaty, *4*

jinn phet: *74*

jiz: in the feelings, *73*

johnnie: strained the cloth of his pants, *39*

journey: *68, 113*; longest, the head is always the, *165*

kanji: from his thirsty tattoo, *87*

Kansas: a fresh deep misery, *83*; packs you tight, *84*

king: *41, 87, 90,120, 149, 153, 172, 179, 230*

kittens: drowned, *37*

kneck: stab himself in the, *69*

laboratory: lie women, moist and humid, vulvas weeping, *164*

labyrinthitis: of the world, *161*

language: as fixed, *145*; as intermediary, *194*; crushed, leaps, *156*; development of, on open plain, *157*; half structured, as an object is half structured, *158*; nothing more real than, *145*; private, *230*; the sadly rumor of, *7*; we could translate but not explain, *198*

laughter: mad, the sign of, *28*

lavender: a crown hive for, *191*

law: *vis-à-vis* Jesus thinking it is not enough, *145*; *vis-à-vis* somebody on the West Wing thinking it is not enough, *145*; that a proposition is not against any, *29*; the, *100*; *vis-à-vis* wearing redblue sweaters with doves stapled onto them, *100*

lawn chairs: *52*

leadership: suspect, under conditions of, *169*

leaves: bleed green into the, *113*; deep-toothed, *109*; felled-tree's, your dresses hang like a, *198*; repleting, and balsams, *86*; roots and, pieces of shell and bone, *200*

ledge: *vis-à-vis* kicking the cotter pin: *172*

leg: Pat Walleck's, *67*; under the cyclone wire concrete, *110*

les fleurs du mal: *164*

les flueurs blanches: *164*

letters: a kind of shielding disguised as whimsy, *176*; dead, secondary duplication in, *154*

light: blinking, warning-planes, *198*; cross-teamed horses of, *192*; God has let there be too much, *85*; *vis-à-vis* inhaling escape, *113*; lake latticed, *86*; negative, as rods and cones turn tactile, *23*; *vis-à-vis* satisfied with reason, *84*; stunned, *90*

lightning: glares on a mangy dog eating his own vomit, *28*

line: *vis-à-vis* his voice quiet and murmuring in my head, *152*; thin, down the back of his neck, *112*

linguist: entombed in North Stacks of library, *157*

living room: Rebecca's, *51*

Louisiana: *189*

love: buckled, *64*; the second object, *197*

lover: *4, 61, 62, 112, 162*

luster: *vis-à-vis* carving a miniature elephant onto the doorknob, *168*

lyric-agonistes: *155*

machine: gives you condoms without paying, *38*

maggots: as meat left in the sun turns to, *23*

magic lantern: *vis-à-vis* Dr. Slatoris, *177*

man: bumping into the same woman, *55*; image of her with another, *147*; miserable miserable, *232*

mannequin: father, in the Sears window, *230*

map: damp spots on his cellar floor, *178*; hand drawn, rotating in different directions: *172*; *vis-à-vis* the past, *78*; maps: at night, she used to read, *89*; straighter than streets, *204*

mark: on the page, bit of clawed mud, *210*; *vis-à-vis* sleeping, *15*

marriage: lasted for a year, *52*; tortured, is going to live a, *147*

mask: blood is flowing to the, *161*; marble apples, *195*; masks: against one another, *25*

maternal: certain weather for the, *32*

maze: hedge, *195*; massive corridor, of PCP, *110*

McQueen pants: *40*

meaning: vanquished, in this efficient use of mourning, *154*

meds: hooked onto the, *69*

megaphone: of sound on water, *66*

melodrama: pure, papier-mâché, *178*

melody: of the connection with they kissed, *73*

member: founding, of a school of poetry, *212*

memory: a teat, calling, *31*; *vis-à-vis* obit going through the wash, *93*; of energy, could wrestle for impersonating, *74*; of Rhea's shameless words, *28*; vs. you, bloody coming up, *8*; memories: panicky, filled with alcohol, *143*

mess: bloody, *169*

message: of linels & sinews, *79*; i don't want October to end the, *106*; messages: read, They have plucked out my teeth, *165*

metal: soft, buckled love, *64*

metaphor: near-diabolical reliance on, *160*; of man's subjection to his dark pleasures, *28*

milk: searching for, tongues pressed to the nipples, *35*; *vis-à-vis* signifying belief in nourishment, *32*

mint marvels: *41*

mistress: dutiful, a spotting scope's, *168*

misunderstanding: slight, this depression, *31*

mode: terrible, of grotesque, *220*

moment: every, hiding in the shadow of, *112*; highway impatient and blind, *93*; research, scholarly in its effort to mine the, *194*; she answers the phone, *53*; moments: appropriate, otherwise feigning death, *100*; odd, of clarity, *183*

monkey: hanging out on the sheer cliff face, *172*; who owned the property, *80*

moon: Ringo Starr inviting to come closer, *226*

morality: strange, I mean where do you get warlords?, *216*

morning: aching thru, *180*; bright contempt, *113*; coiled subway in stations, *220*; of drinking, *10*; person the father calls the next, *53*

mother: entombed alive after giving birth, *35*; etched in the sidewalk, *187*; *vis-à-vis* hoping she will take pity on him, *25*; lying on her back on a hillside covered in nondescript flowers, *23*; *vis-à-vis* Rebecca's father passing away, *51*; *vis-à-vis* the void at the bottom of all that we attempt, *162*; mothers: his two, only then does the fun really begin, *25*

mouth: agape (a gap) as listening as singing, *54*; closed, sewed my, *165*; sewn shut with carpet thread, *18*; *vis-à-vis* stuffing with the primal vox poemato, *90*; the organ who resided, *34*; mouths: vacuous, who carry desire in their, *192*

music: on his skin, as if he were playing the, *5*; unheard, in the dead of his own night, *26*

mutations: morning's inexorable, *180*

muxoxo: *199*

my y ynd: *90*

myrtle: *227*

myth: *vis-à-vis* situating the interpreter, *216*

nails: the day's dirt scraped out from under my, *98*

narratives: movie trailer, *174*

neck: tongue of prior desire, *112*; static when I touched my, *59*; today I am human, *175*

neighbor: *vis-à-vis* arrested for MJ sales and possession, *85*; Ringo Starr, *225*

nerve damage: perminant, *69*

news: pocketed, through the wash, *93*

night: *vis-à-vis* dreaming of their mother dreaming of them, *35*; *vis-à-vis* entertained tragedies, *113*; excess sound at, *13*; in the dead of his own, *26*; last, *83*; Once I lived entirely at, *111*; *vis-à-vis* the girl in the red dress, *57*

nightmare: enjambing with the neighboring information, *174*; stills into an inconvenient, *175*

nihilist: Shakespeare, *146*

nipples: pliable, body damp and lithe, *35*

N-Judah: *137*

noose: protrusions for attaching a, *157*

notebook: blue, labored over, *203*; notebooks: moleskin, *47*

novels: kissing as in, *54*

obedience: thirst's, *34*

obit: Missoulian, phlegm-yellow, *93*

occasion: small, near a sea or wheatfield, *65*

Old Spice: *153*

order: depressive's gesticulation toward, *49*

ordering: conscious, habits of, *154*; reckless, *34*

ordinance: mop 'n glow observatory, *87*

organs: of logic, untamed, *30*

package: to my heroin addict, *103*

padres: grim, *180*

pants: fit me like the skin of an apple, *40*

parchment: *vis-à-vis* bodies softening, *164*

pardon: green car is the key to a, *175*

parlor: *vis-à-vis* waiting to make you wife, *15*

partition: lacy, darkened confessional, *28*

Patriots: your hatred of the, *139*

pattern: each one wants to weave his own into the rug, *63*

pawn: in the game, *234*; pawns: in his crime: *173*

PCP: massive corridor maze of, *110*

penance: page 24 here as, *155*

pence: upon mine staring lidless eye, *89*

penlight: across the clipboard's checkboxes, *88*; studies show the connected thing, *89*

perfume: musk and melon, from Daria's purse, *39*

person: whole, together we are a, *63*

perspective: fresh, rotating the hand drawn map: *172*; in an etching that resembles a water ode, *168*

phat gear: *70*

phenakistoscope: *23*

philosopher: at the top of your game, *215*

picture: *vis-à-vis* father holding me, *52*

pieces: and papers, *47*; and the board's configuration overall, *169*; broken, of plate, *210*; of the sequential film, broken up, *174*

pilgrimage: clumsy, I made my, *67*

pill: injections would serve, *91*; pills: taking, the schedule of, *59*

pillow: blood on my, *9*; to push the body over, *18*

pinwheel crumbs: *41*

pisiform: greyish bruise above the, *8*

pistol: poised, *46*

plaster: casts, of hands feet elbows faces, left by hopers, *67*; *vis-à-vis* the wet contours of her sex, *35*

pleasure: a terrifying hunger for, *22*; had some funny definitions, *149*; strangling, *28*; pleasures: of life, is that enough to sacrifice the other, *232*

pleasure check: cashing in on a, *22*

pocket: secret, *229*; pockets: deep, *vis-à-vis* the coat from Hasbeen thrift store, *38*; full o' theories, *6*

poem: or residence that is a poem, *210*; poems: abandoned like old clothes, *152*

poemato: primal vox, *90*

poetry: the oval sink of, *153*

poker: *vis-à-vis* winning Pat Walleck's leg, *67*

possession: MJ sales and, *85*

post-card writers: *209*

pot: *vis-à-vis* dredlocks, sexual aura, high school, *205*

powder: green, in the tissue paper of this hotel, *99*; *vis-à-vis* grinding for her nose, *90*; licked, turned the bag inside-out, *19*

power: breathless, in this disjunctive synthesis, *162*; went out, *111*

prayer: his stepfather's body genuflected, *18*

prisonhouse: of habit, *154*

privileges: of parasitic priestly class, *157*

professor: and banishment, *145*; of american romanticism, *209*; of Nietzsche, *213*; philosophy, unattractive unless you have joie de vivre, *232*; physics, Dr. Slatoris: *170*

progeny: less than perfect, legacies of, *180*

projection: silent digital, *4*

promise: empty, coiled subway in stations, *220*; made to this new incarnation, *112*

prophylactic: as flesh, aching thru morning's inexorable mutations, *180*

proposals: half-assed, *vis-à-vis* giving them to characters, *212*

protrusions: that could be used for attaching a noose, *157*

pulpits: camouflaged bully, *185*

punchers: brood-blown, the flat gunnels of the, *86*

punks: cigarettes 4, *68*

puss: he felt for my, *40*

Pythagoras: *227*

Qtips: as prose poem, *153*

quantum: *90*

queen: canary, *88*; *vis-à-vis* girl in the fishnet stockings: *172*

Queen: *vis-à-vis* passing the night, *37*

queenie: he called me, when Peter held my hips, *41*

question: halloween forgets, stops being a, *220*; *vis-à-vis* not being able to ask Robert Blake, *230*; only the janitor on work-release had a, *81*

question mark: the scene as a, *26*

rabbit: twitching, of ordinary brutality, *49*

rain: eating toast at the window, *110*; presaged, concomitant with the kindling of flames, *193*; *vis-à-vis* red dress, knee flounce kicked up in the, *98*

rapture: Dr. Slatoris', *177*

reader: *vis-à-vis* the void at the bottom of all we attempt, *162*

reality: crime against: *170, 177*; my supreme assassination, *178*; of the servant, *193*; vs. wishfulness or pandering, *46*

recklessness: acquiring a body by cheating, *31*

red dress: *57*; flesh, rising behind you, *163*; girl, shit-man, I am your, *98*; we bought her, she was in that, shiiiiiiit, *75*

rehab: *143*

relativism: *vis-à-vis* people who want everyone to be a pawn in the game, *234*

relict: bouquet of, *68*

remains: forgotten, rubble piles, *187*

reminiscence: that shiner of a, *3*

retreat: infirm, headlines covering an, *218*; noon, no excuse for a, *112*

rideau street: *220*

river: in a shadow, *114*; Mad, crossed us, *84*; Mad, crossing, *83*; to stand for everything, *66*

riverbank: Pat Walleck, high on the, *67*

road: guess you'll come back down this, *98*; roads: lead you to roaming, *204*

room: crept in, when you dimmed the lights, *204*; is only room, *156*; loom, *vis-à-vis* word-way, *158*; where hopers had left braces, trusses, videotaped mastectomies, *67*; rooms: claustrophobic, closing your eyes in, *195*

roses: fetid, sexes like a field of, *164*

rosewater: *40*

round trips: the insane froth of, *84*

saint medard: convulsionaries of, *17*

sawdust: referential, under evening pumps, *26*

scarf: saw-edged, *167*; scarves: *46*; *vis-à-vis* Robert Blake keeping his face secret, *230*

scene: of a swollen womb, *210*; silent, scabrous, under the sign of mad laughter and convulsive self-consciousness, *28*

schedule: of taking pills, *59*

scientists: nestled between their knees, *164*

secret: dirty, no cover for a, *112*; dirty, suns a, *110*

self: snuff box of, *158*; to abandon any notion of, *162*

self-consciousness: convulsive, *28*; damaged, that part that would have been, *27*; intensive, *vis-à-vis* the crux of my tutelage, *162*; the flash of, *2*

self-defense: strategic, the idea of craftwork as, *194*

self-emulation: exhaustive, to the point of emotional breakdown, *197*

sermon: father yelling in the middle of, *52*

sets: *vis-à-vis* painted carrier doves on walls, *195*; theater, *178*

sex: and crying, *vis-à-vis* Ringo Starr's nightly habits, *225*; maybe we should begin having, *55*; the wet contours of her, the boys finger, *35*; sexes: extracting fluid from, dank as caves, *164*

shadow: of every moment, hiding in the, *112*; state forest, climbing hills into, *93*; shadows: have become a river, *118*; shimmering, a darkened confessional, *28*

Shakespeare: is a nihilist, *146*

shame: and a terrifying hunger for pleasure, *22*; *vis-à-vis* serving as your guide, *162*

she-wolf: and foundling, *35*

shiner: of a reminiscence, *3*

shit: different, real interpretations of, done soberly, *217*; *vis-à-vis* drinking so much and acting like an ass, *143*; infinite, sorry that you carve the, *165*; throw a backward echo on this, *75*; trying to get through the day without losing my, *57*

shoit: only a SAGA-d shooed the, *77*

shutter: that's been making the noise everyone hears and no one can find, *102*

sigh: twinned, across the airshaft, *64*

singularity: absolute absence of, *112*

sink: oval, poetry's, *153*; you will hide in, *100*

sirens: *vis-à-vis* women's bodies, effluvial, *164*

sister: face on the flute, *45*; *vis-à-vis* Robert Blake sign language, *230*

sk8er: *72*

skin: blistering of his, sometimes he could hear the, *112*; in our lives, we who need some, *59*; *21*; peel of a taste of, *175*; playing the music on his, *5*; *vis-à-vis* pulling over head in a long bloody sheet, *162*; raised to meet the blood, *4*; the long border of, *26*

skull cap: *47*

sky: blown like a scrap of paper, *165*; blue, blue is a layer of dust, *175*; part of a promise to this new incarnation, *112*; same, murdering, out of the, *158*; tree &, no longer touch, *118*

Slappy's: that time at, *98*

Sleaze: the rambling splendor, *37*

sleight-of-hand: *vis-à-vis* Dr. Slatoris, *178*; sleights of hand: evermore, why trouble the issue with, *169*

snow: *94, 166, 177*

snuff box: of self, *158*

social segregation: the gories of, *68*

sodaplay: *37*

son: *vis-à-vis* the void at the bottom of all we attempt, *162*; who is all eye, *23*

sound: on water, slow megaphone of, *66*; *vis-à-vis* Pat Walleck falling, *75*

source: slippery, volatile, *160*; divine, kibitzing a: *172*

space: she remembers inhabiting as a child, *16*

space-time: inutile buttocks of, *192*

sparrows: a constellation from apology fields, *191*

spawn, 1/2, 1/2 text, *180*

speaking: vs. writing, *155*

sperm coffin: *102*

spirit: *vis-à-vis* cool chicks arising, *140*

spponoons: cooking up those little, *56*

stage: the world, *vis-à-vis* Dr. Slatoris, *178*

stags: horses more quickly than, *193*

stairs: long steel, *vis-à-vis* Pat Walleck, *67, 75*

star: Hakim, *69*; that he taped to my shirt, *99*; stars: muxoxo, *199*

station: next, me, wounded, approaching at the, *3*; stations: some morning coiled, *220*

statues: *35, 67*

stinger: inserted into the naked back of his stepfather's body, *18*

stockings: fishnet, girl with the ripped: *88, 170, 177*

stone: for lost water, sucking a, *232*; may dream of flight, *90*; water remembers the shape of the, *156*; stones: filling up until he felt swallowed, *200*

storm: *27, 191, 195*

strafings: *183*

stratagem: writing is but speaking's other, *155*

street cred: *71*

student: who begins to seduce the girl far away in Canada, *203*; who found his Missoulian obit, *93*

stump: handless, *201*

suburban pointillism: *45*

subversion: elegant, Dr. Slatoris' most, *178*

suicide: bus rides and, *69*; crosstown away from the, *10*; she threatened the evenings I did not, *64*

suitcase: *41, 42*

sun: blazing mercilessly into the morning, *113*; crossing our backs like a river, *117*; *vis-à-vis* feeling like demise, *200*; *vis-à-vis* meat turning to maggots, *23*; muscled in, *54*; on top of all this, *98*; which adds up to them, *111*

sunlight: dirty, gushing into her, *23*; mango tree, her metal cage or, *110*

surviving: one piece in the process of, *173*

SUV: parked, mutating like cells in a, *180*

taste: of skin, *175*

teardrop: at the base of my ass, *40*

tears: Ringo Starr's, *225*

teeth: eye, the loosening of, *62*; plucked out my, *165*; the moon's, *204*

Tegrin: as prose poem, *153*

temptation: to not betray his mother, *28*

tension: of the possible storm, *27*

text: 1/2, 1/2 spawn, *180*; blankets an old regime, *160*; disjunctive, has its charms, *169*; pg. 24 buried in, *159*

Thelonious Monk: my ass, *136*

thighs: the bone corset-stays, *163*; women's, hands part the, *164*

thrift store: Hasbeen, *38*

throat: aware of a sudden ache there, *26*; *vis-à-vis* berries sliding down, *200*; crammed with bees as far down as he could reach, *20*; fiercest, scene of a swollen womb or swallowed by, *210*; *vis-à-vis* mother's gesture making his heart leap in his, *25*; suspense in my, *39*

time: and space, a merging of, *113*; getting past, *63*; kickoff, *99*; *vis-à-vis* pg. 24 & pg. 24 being identical, *153*; photographed, *198*; strange sense of, he too must experience the, *103*; strange sense of, libidinal economy's, *22*; to situate the interpreter, *216*

tits: the goal of America, *235*

toast: *75, 87, 110, 112*

tongue: cut out my, *165*; of prior desire, *112*; tongues: nascent, wolves that speak in, *192*; pressed to the nipples, searching for milk, *35*; what they mime, *37*

tragedies: all of the comedies would be, *146*; the night had entertained, *113*

trance state: with a desire to be in a, *150*

trap: to be sprung, *151*

travertine: molding their mother's body out of, *35*

trolley girl: *58*

trusses: the other hopers had left, *67*

tutelage: crux of my, *162*

unadvantagetakers: *57*

uncertainty: narrator's, and the utter void of his fear, *162*

underwear: and old Boy Scout awards, *19*

underworld: a dark hallway littered with debris, *16*

uterine walls: scraping and excisscating the, *164*

vacillation: paradoxical, between self-dissolution and intensive self-consciousness, *162*

vampire: *65*

variations: treetop, gentle, the dead fish in his head, *110*

veins: emptying, *8*

vesitigal sense: in the hours alone, *65*

vessel: the cup when thirsty, *154*

vicadin: *68*

vice: *vis-à-vis* resembling his mother, *28*

virgin: *35, 41*

voice: box, chain-gang, toilet bowl finger tuck, *165*; his, quiet and murmuring in my head, *152*; rides the length of me, *8*

vomit: mangy dog eating his own, *28*

vulvas: weeping, *164*

warlords: *216*

water: birds open beaked on the, *66*; frozen, not to look over the, *94*; lost, sucking a stone for, *232*; only, *198*; *vis-à-vis* offering to the law, *100*; pistol, *46*; quest for quarries dried of, *60*; remembering the shape of the stone, *156*; slow, Pat Walleck watching us across the, *67*; *vis-à-vis* the black line, *189*; *vis-à-vis* the ecstasy of saints, *16*; the moon's teeth loud on the, *204*; why is there, *65*; women suspended above the, *164*

West Wing: *145*

wet shrine: *28, 164*

wheatfield: sea or, a small occasion near a, *65*

whip: that little bitching according her, *4*

whisper hairlash: in your eye you keep pullin at, *98*

whispering: in your kitchen cupboards, *168*

white trash: *72*

whorehouses: *78*

wigga: *71*

willpower: *vis-à-vis* rehab, *143*

wind: *21, 39, 90, 210*

window: bedroom, broken, *190*; on birdsex, *110*; or still, if chalk rolls through the, *156*; rain eating toast at the, *110*; stack yourself against the, *8*; wreck remembered film marks lifting a, *191*

windowsill: wet toast on the, *112*; windowsills: greasy, wipin' down, *98*

wind-up key: *vis-à-vis* Dr. Slatoris, *178*

winter: *43, 189*

wire: cyclone, part of his leg under, *110*; shut my eyes with, *165*; wires: wet, fallen birds, *195*

wolves: *166, 192*

woman: filthy, *vis-à-vis* Ringo Starr's sexual proclivity, *225*; same, man keeps bumping into the, *55*; who fingered her necklace, *165*; women: moist and humid, vulvas weeping, *164*; very attractive, I have been able, in my life, to sleep with, *205*; willing, along streets with, *9*

womb: *35, 210*

word: every, an unnecessary stain, *101*; lawful, *30*; she reclaims the, *50*; words: estranged, *152*; he's written for the older woman, *203*; I was fit to burst with, *61*; shameless, the memory of Rhea's, *28*; your, were like blinds, *165*

work: defined by its desperate strangeness, *149*; scholarly in its effort to mine the research moment, *194*

work-release: the janitor on, *81*

wreck: remembered film marks lifting a window, *191*

wrist: back of the, breaking its wing, *111*; tagged at the, *42*; wrists: refuse to bend, snap the way, *5*

writer: *vis-à-vis* this void at the bottom of all that we attempt, *162*; with the corpse, *193*

writing: breaking ground, a piece of, *159*; speaking's other stratagem, not to be tread upon, *155*; *vis-à-vis* provoking a mood swing, *169*

yard: & blo up the back of the, *68*; I let him into the, *189*; old, he thought about his, *112*

yearbook: *194*

yolk: like dirty sunlight gushing into her, *23*

yuou: *56*

zero: like after like, as harsh as, *84*

zipper: metal teeth parting, *40*

zoozoos: in the kitchen, *74*

Zyprexa: *88*

Jenny Allan
Halt & Hither • 3, 84

A.K. Arkadin
For Robert Blake's Sake • 229

Jeff Bacon & Francis Raven
if what can change then everything can change •
138, 205, 211, 215, 232

Andrea Baker
River • 66
Gather • 94

Julia Bloch
from *Letters to Kelly Clarkson* • 43, 45, 49, 61

Lawrence Ytzhak Braithwaite
Pull Your Ears Back • 69
Turntable Interrogation Techniques • 120

Nick Bredie
Camera & Properties • 23, 161, 163

Amina Cain
from *Watching a Bird Fight as Person* • 44

Kate Hill Cantrill
Dear all mouses, • 60

Nona Caspers
from *A Book of One Hundred Days* • 207, 223, 224

Jimmy Chen
Give Pete a Chance • 136

Kim Chinquee
Our Fathers • 51

John Cleary
dear jack, • 56

Steve Dalachinsky
cecil taylor - derek bailey duo @ tonic 5/3/00 • 5
cecil taylor trio @ the bluenote 7/19/05 • 76
cecil taylor trio @ castle clinton 7/29/04 • 114
Category 5 • 182

Catherine Daly
from *Discretionary (Virtual)* • 37
from *Discretionary (Paper)* • 50

Brett Evans & Chris Stroffolino
Mercenary Beverages • 68

Brian Evenson
Stung • 18
Scene • 25
Esquisse • 162

Raymond Farr
"Pg. 24" a Pseudo-Litany, Being Lines Written By Anon. • 152
Dear Nadine, • 155
Journal Entry: 12-26-05 • 158
Opus Californium • 180

Sandy Florian
And your messages • 165
24 • 193

Paul Gacioch
When the Law Comes • 100
Sweet Ringo • 225

Anne Germanacos
Students • 200

Scott Glassman
Aegean Redux • 87

Noah Eli Gordon & Joshua Marie Wilkinson
from *Figures For a Darkroom Voice* • 168, 191

Paul Hardacre
from *The river is far behind us* • 110

HL Hazuka
Dear Grady, • 98
Still • 186

Anne Heide
from *Wiving* • 12

Malia Jackson
Postcards From a Family Roadtrip Through the American West •
82, 95, 96, 97

Carrie-Sinclair Katz
from *Meanwhile (a Movement Missive Series)* •
8, 62, 64, 83, 101

Susanna Kittredge
Conservatory of Flowers • 86
Church Street • 219

Richard Kostelanetz
Full Moon at Arverne • 181
Arverne Hotel • 228

Kristine Leja
Here Is Where • 47

Norman Lock
The King and the Cotter Pin • 177

Doug MacPherson
24 • 199

Scott Malby
24 • 227

Bob Marcacci
from *Excess Conceptions Meditations Rapist* • 104

Bill Marsh
from *Dead Letter Game* • 154, 160, 169, 176, 194, 197

rob mclennan
still • 156
neck • 175
grotesque • 220

LJ Moore
from *Between* • 134

Greg Mulcahy
Picayune • 149

Cathi Murphy
The Man Who Ate Breakfast for Dinner • 112

Eireene Nealand
No Excuse for the Tension of a Possible Storm •
27, 63, 85, 92, 103
Dear Lo, • 99

Daniel Pendergrass
Market Street & McAllister • 218

Kristin Prevallet
Orphée • 16

kathryn l. pringle
BART ii. head bandage replete with hole • 42
mission st & 19th st with grey gardens • 46

Stephen Ratcliffe
from *Painting* • 53

Francis Raven & Jeff Bacon
if what can change then everything can change •
138, 205, 211, 215, 232

AE Reiff
Ailin Penlight • 89

Daniel C. Remein
film professor with beautiful hands • 192
from *keystone service letters* • 209

Elizabeth Robinson
from *Proposition* • 29

Zach Savich
Photograph in which everything is blurred • 54
Sing/Le Figure • 167
Composition 24 • 195
23:59 • 198

Len Shneyder
Sutro Heights • 204

Nina Shope
Three Fragments • 17, 35, 164

Kyle Simonsen
listen bro, • 75

Ed Skoog
Pat Walleck's Leg • 67
The World-Famous Topeka Zoo • 81
Dog Highway • 93
Season Finale • 189

Jason Snyder
from *The Fall* • 1, 10

Anna Joy Springer
The Forest of Clashing Erotics • 24

Chris Stroffolino & Brett Evans
Mercenary Beverages • 68

Cole Swensen
They • 111
It Is Wrong • 166

Joanne Tracy
Queenie • 38

Chris Tysh
from *Mother, I* • 4, 22, 26, 28

Nico Vassilakis
Punct • 196

James Wagner
from *Reynolds—part one of Claims of Unmanned
Aerial Vehicles* • 9, 55, 65, 102, 174, 214, 222

Derek White
Controlled Sledding in Theory • 36
Airborne Spear Contraception • 133
Post-Holing to the Flesh Temple • 170
Fijian Field Data • 221

Joshua Marie Wilkinson & Noah Eli Gordon
from *Figures For a Darkroom Voice* • 168, 191

Angela Woodward
Lost Languages • 157

EPISTOLARY
09.01.05

Epistolary, Sidebrow's inaugural project, was launched to establish a forum for collaboration, one with multiple senders and recipients, as well as interpenetrating correspondence, in mind. Direct address, elegy, and on-page collaboration are among the alternate epistolary forms thus far explored. Response, especially explorations of threads and relationships already under way, is highly encouraged (www.sidebrow.net/2006/epistolary.php).

3, 8, 9, 27, 36, 43, 45, 49, 55, 56, 60, 61, 62, 63, 64, 65, 67, 68, 75, 82, 83, 84, 85, 92, 93, 95, 96, 97, 98, 99, 100, 101, 102, 103, 133, 138, 155, 156, 165, 174, 175, 182, 189, 205, 209, 211, 214, 215, 220, 221, 222, 232

LITOPOLIS
09.01.05

Launched as a means for establishing an aesthetic geography of San Francisco, Litopolis has since expanded to include New York, with additional cities and regions on the way (www.sidebrow.net/2006/litopolissf.php). Litopolis uses cartography as a framework for the arrangement of pieces in an effort to explore how differing aesthetic visions co-habitat when placed almost incidentally side by side. It is as much an experiment in how tagging creative expression with specific location affects the work's reception as it is an investigation of how tagging location with creative expression alters the environs.

1, 5, 10, 24, 42, 46, 47, 76, 86, 114, 134, 136, 186, 204, 207, 218, 219, 223, 224

PAGE 24
11.15.05

Spun from a thought posed by grady in John Cleary's "dear jack," (page 56), Page 24 explores the notion of a book comprised entirely of page 24s. The project thus far includes extant and reimagined page 24s of works-in-progress, formal manipulations of the number 24, retranslations of 24th poems, musings on the 24th page of books both real and imagined, and so on. The project remains open to interpretation (www.sidebrow.net/2006/page24.php).

37, 44, 50, 54, 152, 155, 157, 158, 167, 180, 193, 195, 196, 198, 199, 227

MOTHER, I
01.31.06

Inspired by Sidebrow's first post, excerpts of Chris Tysh's screenplay adaptation of Georges Bataille's *Mother, I* (pages 4, 22, 26, 28), Mother, I is a multi-author, multi-genre foray into the maternal, in large part shaded by the dark, erotic prescriptiveness of the mother figure in Bataille. The project is open to response, reimaginings, and inquiries into the maternal beyond Bataille (www.sidebrow.net/2006/motheri.php).

4, 12, 16, 17, 18, 22, 23, 24, 25, 26, 28, 29, 35, 98, 161, 162, 163, 164, 165, 192

POST-HOLE
04.10.06

Prompted by Derek White's "Post-Holing to the Flesh Temple" (page 170), Post-Hole is a multi-author, multi-genre menagerie of grotesques. With posts that allude to contexts and characters in other pieces, as Norman Lock's "The King and the Cotter Pin" (page 177) does directly, and the possibility of Dr. Slatoris lurking throughout, this project provides ample opportunity for shaping the mystery of Post-Hole (www.sidebrow.net/2006/posthole.php).

38, 69, 81, 87, 89, 112, 149, 154, 156, 160, 169, 170, 175, 176, 177, 194, 197, 200, 220, 225, 229

OUR FATHERS
03.26.07

Kim Chinquee's "Our Fathers" (page 51) initiated this complement to Mother, I. The project, with the paternal recurring, is in its early stages, open to new directions, response, and reinterpretations (www.sidebrow.net/2006/ourfathers.php).

12, 16, 51, 53, 229

GHOST
04.09.07

Submitted alongside "They" (page 111) and "It Is Wrong" (page 116), Cole Swensen's suggestion of a project involving ghosts shed light on pieces previously posted to the Sidebrow site. As much an aesthetic and formal mood as it an investigation in the disembodied and envoiced, Ghost remains open to interpretation (www.sidebrow.net/2006/ghost/php).

66, 94, 104, 110, 111, 166, 168, 181, 191, 228